Dream Power
for Teens

What your dreams say about
your past, present, and future

Rob MacGregor

ADAMS MEDIA
AVON, MASSACHUSETTS

Published by Adams Media,
an F+W Publications Company
57 Littlefield Street, Avon, MA 02322. U.S.A.
www.adamsmedia.com

ISBN: 1-59337-024-5

Printed in Canada.

J I H G F E D C B A

Library of Congress Cataloging-in-Publication Data
MacGregor, Rob.
Dream power for teens / Rob MacGregor.
p.   cm.
Summary: A comprehensive guide to understanding
and harnessing the power of dreams.
ISBN 1-59337-024-5
1. Teenagers' dreams. [1. Dreams. 2. Dream interpretation.] I. Title.
BF1099.T43M23   2004
154.6'3--dc22   2003022386

This publication is designed to provide accurate and authoritative information
with regard to the subject matter covered. It is sold with the understanding
that the publisher is not engaged in rendering legal, accounting, or other
professional advice. If legal advice or other expert assistance is required, the
services of a competent professional person should be sought.
       —From a *Declaration of Principles* jointly adopted by a Committee of the
American Bar Association and a Committee of Publishers and Associations

Many of the designations used by manufacturers and sellers to distinguish
their product are claimed as trademarks. Where those designations appear in
this book and Adams Media was aware of a trademark claim, the designations
have been printed with initial capital letters.

This book is available at quantity discounts for bulk purchases.
For information, call 1-800-872-5627.

Dedication

To Trish and Megan

Acknowledgments

I'd like to thank Byron Brunskill for giving his seventh- and eighth-grade language arts students at Polo Park Middle School in Wellington, Florida, the assignment to remember and record their dreams. Many of those dreams found their way into this text.

Contents

Contents

Introduction

Dreamscape

The dream world is the real world.
—SENECA INDIAN HEALER

In the dream, you're watching a drama that is taking place in an emergency room. There's lots of action, with doctors and nurses rushing around. Suddenly you realize that you're not just watching what's happening—somehow, you're part of the drama. Just as you start to wonder what you're doing here, the scene shifts. Now you're at the mall with a bunch of your friends. Even though everything looks different, it still feels like the emergency room. People are running around, moving so fast. Things are not right—the stairs to the second level go halfway up and just stop, in midair. Mall security guards seem to be everywhere. You can't find your friends. You feel lost and confused. You wake up gasping for air, your forehead wet with sweat, your heart pounding.

The next morning, as you get ready for school, you think about your dream. You try to remember it, but by the time you've finished your cereal, it has already started to fade. No big deal; you just go about your day. You've got a lot on your mind—an English quiz third period and a job interview after school. They're hiring down at the ice cream shop in the mall. By lunchtime, you find you can't remember the dream at all—only the strange feeling you had when you woke up.

But hey, listen up. Whether you know it or not, your dreams can often give you clues about what is going on in your life. They can give you a different perspective on the people you know, your family and friends, even the fears you may have. By paying attention to the insight provided in your dreams, you can empower yourself. If you learn to remember your dreams and begin to record them, you'll find that certain symbols and patterns are repeated. By studying and analyzing them, you'll inadvertently embark on a fabulous journey of self-discovery.

The dream above is real. It was recorded by a sixteen-year-old girl looking for her first job. It could reflect her emotional turmoil about the bewildering process of finding that job. She was aware that she would be starting at the bottom—the first level—and, as those incomplete stairs indicated, she was cut off from high-paying jobs because of her inexperience and the need to continue her education.

In *Dream Power for Teens,* you'll learn techniques for remembering and recording your dreams as well as information you can use to interpret them. You'll discover that you can "incubate" dreams—that is, request dreams about your life before you fall asleep. You can explore the meaning of nightmares and find out about advanced skills, such as lucid dreaming and even out-of-body dreams. You'll find a chapter on common dream themes, like falling or flying, or arriving in class totally unprepared for a test. One whole chapter is devoted to sharing your dreams with friends. Dream groups provide a chance for you to improve your dreaming and dream interpretation skills. They give you the opportunity to help others with their dreams and get help with your own.

Each chapter includes exercises to help you work with your dreams. The more you learn about dreams, the more meaningful they can become. Take a look at the glossary of interpretations at the back of the book. That's where you can get immediate feedback on images in your dreams.

About the Author

I've always had an active dream life. In fact, on a good night I might record as many as eight dreams. I've been keeping regular track of them for more than two decades. I've noticed that I often dream about traveling, either by bus or train or plane. In particular, I seem to take a lot of trains in my dreams, definitely more than I do in waking life. Sometimes I fumble around with my luggage. I worry that I'm going to lose it, and I dash to make the train on time. So my dream journeys, just like life's journeys, are not always smooth and effortless. If there's a message in these dreams, I guess it would be that I'm still in training.

Along the way I've written two other dream books. I coauthored *The Everything® Dreams Book* (Adams Media) with my wife, Trish, and I wrote *The Pocket Dream Dictionary* (Running Press). I also wrote an astrology book with my teen daughter, Megan. It's called *Star Power for Teens* (Career Press).

Besides my nonfiction books, I've written seventeen novels, including two mystery novels for young adults. *Prophecy Rock* won the Edgar Allan Poe award in the young adult category, and *Hawk Moon* was a finalist for the award. I also wrote a series of adventure novels featuring Indiana Jones. The first one was based on the movie script of *Indiana Jones and the Last Crusade.*

Now, before we get into our dreams, let's talk a little about sleep, the nighttime realm where dreams materialize like movies on the screen of your mind's eye.

Part 1

Working with Your Dreams

Myths are public dreams, dreams are private myths.
—JOSEPH CAMPBELL, AMERICAN MYTHOLOGIST

One

The Way of Sleep

I should have lost many a good hit, had I not set down at once things that occurred to me in my dreams.

—Sir Walter Scott

Imagine falling asleep one night and not waking up again for twenty-five years. It would seem like you'd slept your life away. You would have missed everything! Your friends would be all grown up with kids of their own, but you hadn't even finished high school.

Actually, you *will* sleep for years—many years, but not all at once.

Who has time to sleep away one whole third of their life? You're probably not even tired at ten or eleven o'clock. You still feel wide awake, even though you've gotta get up for school. It doesn't make any difference if your parents hassle you about staying up too late. Even when you go to bed early, you just lay there staring at the ceiling for what seems like hours. And getting up early the next morning is probably harder than falling asleep.

Nighttime Notes

By the time you turn seventy-five, you will probably have spent twenty-five years of your life asleep.

The good news is that you're not being weird or abnormal. You're just responding to your biological clock, which determines when we sleep and when we are awake. This "clock" consists of a group of 10,000 cells located deep within the brain, in the hypothalamus. It responds to darkness and light. It usually clicks into the waking mode when you're in bright light and into the sleep mode when it's dark.

You've probably heard that saying attributed to Benjamin Franklin, "Early to bed, early to rise makes a man healthy, wealthy and wise." Ben obviously didn't know about the biological sleep cycles of teenagers when he penned that ditty.

Nighttime Notes

As a teen, your brain tends to run on a later cycle than adults. But teens aren't allowed to sleep later, because high schools traditionally begin classes at seven or eight in the morning. As a result, many teens are sleepy during the day. Even though you still need as much or more sleep than preteens, the average teen gets between six and seven hours of sleep a night.

But, hey, let's face it. If you're sleepy during the day, it can affect your grades, your health, and your happiness. Sleep-deprived people tend to be sad, irritable, and impatient. Even being just a little sleepy can hurt your performance in everything from test-taking to playing sports video games. "How we deal with stressful situations during the day may have a lot to do with how much sleep we're getting," says Dr. Phyllis Zee, director of the sleep disorder center at Northwestern University Medical School.

Get Your ZZZs...

Here are some tips from the National Sleep Foundation to help you get more sleep:

* Try to go to bed and wake up at about the same time every day, even on weekends and vacations. That way your biological clock won't get disrupted.

✳ Try to stick to your schedule. If you have to break it, get back on track right away—in one or two nights, at most. Don't stay up past your bedtime by more than an hour, and get up within two hours of when you normally would. If you're sleepy during the day, take an afternoon nap.

✳ Learn how much sleep you need to be at your best. Many teens need between eight and a half and nine and a half hours each night. If you need nine hours, figure out what time you should go to bed by calculating back from the time you have to get up.

✳ Get into bright light as soon as possible in the morning, but avoid it in the evening. Different light levels help to signal the brain when it should be awake and when it should be ready to go to sleep.

✳ Cut down on the fluids you drink before going to sleep.

✳ If you get sleepy at a particular time during the day, see if you can arrange your schedule so that you get involved in stimulating activities, like a computer game, at that time of the day. (That might be easier said than done, but it's worth mentioning, in case you do have some flexibility in your schedule.)

✳ Colas and other beverages that contain caffeine can keep you awake at night. It's a good idea to stay away from them in the evening.

✳ Chill out before going to bed. Relax, read, take a bath. Stay away from computer games and other activities that stimulate your mind. Don't fall asleep with the television on, either. The flickering light can result in restless sleep.

✳ Say no to all-nighters. Staying up late messes up your sleep patterns. You'll feel horrible the next day, and it'll take awhile to get back on a regular sleep schedule.

✳ Get your friends involved in keeping tabs on their sleep habits. See who gets the most sleep and who gets the least. Who feels best?

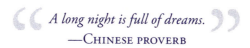

A long night is full of dreams.
—CHINESE PROVERB

Tracking Your Sleep

Keep track of your sleep schedule for two weeks. Afterwards, divide the total by the number of days you recorded your sleep time, and you've got your average.

	Bedtime	Wake Time	Total Hours	Am I Rested?
Sunday				
Monday				
Tuesday				
Wednesday				
Thursday				
Friday				
Saturday				
Sunday				
Monday				
Tuesday				
Wednesday				
Thursday				
Friday				
Saturday				

Average hours of sleep per night:

Dream Time

The longer you sleep each night, the more dreams you will have. The longest dreams and the easiest ones to remember usually come near the end of a full night's sleep. To understand how you dream, you have to understand the four stages of sleep.

Nighttime Notes

During a typical night, you pass through four distinct phases of sleep. These are distinguished by the frequency of your brain waves, your eye movement, and the degree of your muscle tension.

Stage One

During the first sleep stage, your brain is shifting out of its normal waking state. Your brain waves have certain rhythms. Your waking state is called "beta." As you fall asleep, your brain waves shift to an "alpha" pattern, oscillating between eight and twelve cycles a second. Your heart and pulse rates, blood pressure, and body temperature drop slightly. Your muscles begin to relax, and you experience drifting sensations. Surreal images—usually having something to do with your last thoughts or some aspect of your life—may flit through your mind. These are called hypnagogic images, and they are often extremely vivid. Even though they are brief, they can be as significant as longer dreams in a deeper stage of sleep.

Stage Two

In the second sleep stage, you drift into a light slumber. Your brain waves now register a "theta" pattern, which is characterized by rapid bursts of brain activity. They look like spindles when they're recorded by an electroencephalogram. (See diagram.) Most of our dreams occur in the second stage. If you watch someone sleeping, you can actually see her dream, because her eyes move back and forth beneath her eyelids. This period of rapid eye movement, or REM, usually lasts for several minutes at a time during stage two.

Brain Wave Frequencies

Name	Brain Wave Frequency	State of Consciousness
Beta	14 to 30 cps	Fully awake, alert, excitement, tension
Alpha	8 to 12 cps	Deeply relaxed, passive awareness, composed
Theta	4 to 7 cps	Drowsiness, unconscious, tranquility, dreaming
Delta	.5 to 3.5 cps	Deep sleep, lack of awareness
Deep delta	.5 to 2 cps	Deep unconsciousness

cps = cycles per second

Stages Three and Four

Twenty to forty-five minutes after you drift off into sleep, you move into the third level of sleep. Now your brain waves start to register large, slow "delta" waves, which indicate deep sleep. In the fourth stage, the percentage of delta waves continues to increase, as you go into an even deeper level of sleep. If someone tries to wake you up during this stage, you will be disoriented and want to go back to sleep immediately.

After up to an hour of deep delta sleep, you return to the third stage of sleep, and then you come back to the stage two, or theta. This is the stage where you dream the most, and where someone watching could tell you were in REM sleep from the movement of your eyes. This time, your blood pressure rises, your pulse quickens, and your brain waves become similar to those when you're awake. This first REM period lasts five to ten minutes. Each time the REM period is repeated, it lasts longer. The final one of the night might extend for a full hour.

At best, you spend about 20 percent of your sleeping time in theta, during which time you might have several dreams.

Nighttime Notes

During a lifetime, you might experience more than a 100,000 dreams. How many of those are remembered, of course, varies greatly from person to person. But we do know that if you are interested in remembering and understanding your dreams, you'll remember more and more of them.

Dream Types

Just as movies can be categorized into genres, such as dramas, comedies, action-adventure, or horror—there are different kinds of dreams, too.

The Mind Cool-Down

"Cool down" dreams repeatedly go over something that happened during your day. For example, if you were intensely involved in a sport, or you took a difficult test, or you did the same thing again and again, like bagging groceries at the supermarket after school, then you might dream about it. That's just the mind's way of dealing with the day's activities. Usually, you don't remember many of these dreams, but when you do, you can easily connect them with activities in your life.

The Problem-Solver

Your subconscious—the part of your mind that lies below your conscious awareness—knows all about your problems, and it usually knows how to solve them even if you don't. If the subconscious thinks its solution is important enough, you'll be given a problem-solving dream. You can usually recognize these dreams by the feelings that come with them. You might feel a "zing" of recognition, or you might get chills or goose bumps.

Nighttime Notes

You should be able to link the message of the dream to your problem. But even if you don't remember it when you wake up, you might come up with a similar solution that just pops into your head.

Take the example of thirteen-year-old Janice, whose parents are divorced. Her fifteen-year-old brother, Ben, teased her relentlessly, day after day. He was mad about the divorce and took it out on her because she was the one person in the family he could control. Janice was miserable, but her mother said she was tired of hearing about her problems with Ben.

In her dream, Janice was talking with her father, who lived in another state and had a girlfriend. He was apologizing for any problems he had caused her and asked if there was anything he could do to help. When she woke up, Janice knew she needed to call her dad, even though her mother always said he was too busy with his new life to do much with them. All it took was a five-minute conversation, and after that, her father asked her to put Ben on the phone. The two of them had a long private talk, and that evening Ben apologized to her. Things got much better after that.

The Psych Job

Psychological dreams are ones that bring subconscious "junk" to the surface. Instead of helping us solve a problem or make a decision, these dreams make us face something about ourselves that might be blocking us from moving forward.

Nighttime Notes

Psych dreams are often about our scarier feelings, such as our inner fears, anxieties, insecurities, guilt, and resentment. Some of them are nightmares, and others are extremely vivid. You could say that they are the "horror" genre of dreaming. Sometimes they are repetitive, like a movie you keep going back to see over and over again. It's probably the subconscious telling you to wake up and listen.

Sixteen-year old Rick dreamed about snakes after moving to Phoenix, Arizona:

"I'm walking along a path and snakes are slithering away. I'm afraid I'll step on a poisonous one and it'll bite me. Then one of them suddenly drops from a tree in front of me and I wake up gasping for air."

Rick's on a new path in a new school, and he has some fears about it. The dream might be revealing his fears about his new situation. But snakes, which shed their skins, can also represent wisdom and transformation. Rick is undergoing a personal transformation brought on by the changes. On the other hand, such dreams might also be realistic warnings rather than symbolic. For example, the dream could be alerting Rick to the presence of poisonous snakes near where he lives. Only Rick can determine the best way of interpreting the dream.

The Crystal Ball

Then there are precognitive dreams, in which you see an event before it happens.

For instance, you dream about an old friend, and the next day you run into her, even though you haven't see each other for months. Or you dream that you are signing

Nighttime Notes

The word "precognitive" literally means "to know ahead."

the cast on the arm of a neighborhood kid and a couple of days later, you happen to see the kid in the tree house next door. You remember the dream. You hesitate, then decide to warn him. He laughs and tells you you're too late. Then you see he's already wearing a cast, and he says he broke his wrist yesterday playing basketball. "Do you want to sign it?" he asks.

Many precognitive dreams, however, aren't that straightforward. The message is often revealed through symbols, which makes them challenging to interpret. Your dream of a grown-up handing you a gift-wrapped package might not link up right away to your math teacher, who gave you an A for the quarter when you expected a B. Usually, you can detect these dreams by their strange quality. The lighting might be off, either too dim or noticeably bright, or objects might be oddly shaped or made of peculiar materials. While precognitive dreams may not occur very often, when they do, they are worth pursuing.

Just a Bunch of Nonsense?

If you start working with your dreams and talking about them, you may run across teachers, parents, or friends who say that dreams are meaningless or dumb. They may say that you're wasting your time recording and interpreting them. But you can learn a lot of cool stuff about yourself from your dreams.

So why do some people dis dreams? The study of dreams is subjective. Objective truth is the kind of thing that can be counted and categorized, such as the number of people in your family, their age, sex, and weight. Subjective truth relies on things that can't be measured or weighed. Just like music appreciation, a love of sports, or even some kinds of science, like psychology, dream study depends on your personal interpretation. After all, you're not counting beans. In fact, there's a saying that goes, "Everything that counts can't be counted."

Actually, scientists know very little about dreaming. James Pagel, M.D., chairman of the dreams section of the American Sleep Disorder Association, readily acknowledges that fact. "Dreaming is still a very limited science. We don't even know why people sleep, let alone why they dream."

Working with Your Dreams

Here are a few questions to consider about the nature of your dreams. You may not be able to answer many of the questions right away, but after working with your dreams for a while, you just might find that your answers change dramatically.

- How many dreams do you remember a week?
- Which of the four dream types do you think you have most often: Processing? Problem solving? Psychological? Precognitive?
- Can you remember any processing dreams that related to your day's activities?
- What were you doing?
- Have you ever solved a problem as a result of information in a dream? If so, what was it?

- Can you recall any psychological dreams that opened up any fears or worries or insecurities? Were they nightmares or just vivid dreams?
- Have you ever had a precognitive dream in which something you dreamed about really happened? Describe it so you won't forget about it.

Lion

A driving force, sense of power, victory. If the lion is chasing you, the indication is that you are vulnerable to attack. A caged lion implies that you will be successful as long as the opposition is held in check. Alternately, a lion can represent a male authority figure, someone you look up to or fear. In astrology, Leo the lion is a fire sign, a symbol of courage, confidence, recognition, and personal magnetism.

Two

Masterful Dreamers

Are not the sane and insane equal at night
as the sane lies dreaming?
—CHARLES DICKENS

Even though dreams may sometimes seem like a confusing jumble of nonsensical images, those who have listened to their dreams throughout history have found otherwise. Among them are many famous scientists, inventors, and writers.

Nighttime Notes

As a teenager, Albert Einstein dreamed he was flying a sled through the sky at faster and faster speeds. When he reached a certain speed, the stars changed shapes and glowed in fantastic colors. He never forgot the dream, and thinking about it, years later, he was inspired to develop his greatest accomplishment—the theory of relativity. In other words, $E = mc^2$ is something he literally "dreamed up."

Problem-solving dreams helped many famous people find the key to their invention, discovery, or scientific breakthrough.

Elias Howe invented the sewing machine needle after a dream in which he was attacked by natives brandishing spears with holes in the ends. Keep in mind, though, that Howe didn't just happen upon these breakthrough dreams without any preparation. He was deeply involved in his field when his dream occurred. So his problem-solving dream provided guidance on a matter in which he was seeking answers.

Reading a scary story at bedtime might cause nightmares, but nightmares may also cause scary stories. Mary Shelley dreamed about a monster made by a mad scientist and wrote *Frankenstein*. The author Robert Louis Stevenson dreamed many of his stories. He claimed that he could go back to his story night after night and pick it up where he left off. He could even dream stories on demand when he needed to sell one. One of his most famous, *The Strange Case of Dr. Jekyll and Mr. Hyde,* was the result of such a dream. He asked for a story as he went to sleep so he could pay his bills. After two nights, he dreamed of a man who was a double being—one kind and gentle, the other monstrous.

Nighttime Notes

Great writers = smart dreamers. Be sure to keep up with your dream journal.

Stevenson and Shelley have plenty of company among storytellers. In interviews with San Francisco radio host Naomi Epel, twenty-six well-known novelists, among them Anne Rice, Stephen King, Sue Grafton, Amy Tan, and William Styron, all described how their dreams have influenced their work.

The Sleeping Prophet

One of the most unusual masters of dreaming was an uneducated man from Kentucky named Edgar Cayce (1877–1944). Cayce would take a nap in a comfortable chair and talk in his sleep when people asked him questions. The answers came from a place deep within himself where he connected with what he called "universal consciousness" or "cosmic mind."

In his sleep state, he could not only answer people's questions, he could also make medical diagnoses using medical terms he didn't know when he was fully awake. The person could be in the room with Cayce or a thousand miles away. It didn't matter to him. He could speak foreign languages he had never learned and get information he had no access to in his waking life.

As a result of his amazing abilities, he received more than one invitation to the White House. At one time, he worked with six doctors assisting them in their diagnosis of patients, and he always did so in a sleep state. For more information on the remarkable dream life of Edgar Cayce, you can visit the Cayce Web site listed in the appendix.

Edgar Cayce thought that the meaning of the symbols in dreams varied from person to person. But in examining his readings on dreams, he found that certain common meanings did emerge:

- Animals: Man's negative and positive qualities. The wilder the animal, the more primitive the emotion.
- A boat: Life's journey.
- Fire: A cleansing, wrath, or destruction.
- Fish: Christ, spirituality, spiritual journey, or spiritual forces.
- Fishing: Man's search for higher consciousness.
- A house: The body, the self.
- Mud or tangled weeds: A need for cleansing, purification.
- Nudity: Exposure or vulnerability to the criticism of others.
- Snake: Wisdom, primal desires.
- Water: The unconscious, the source of life, or a spiritual journey.

The Psychology of Dreaming

Unlike Edgar Cayce, psychologists Sigmund Freud and Carl Jung aren't particularly known for their dreams. Rather, they are renowned for what they *said* about dreams. The two men have had the greatest impact on the way we look at dreams.

Sigmund Freud (1856–1939) opened the door to the scientific study of dreams with his book *The Interpretation of Dreams* in 1899. Freud believed that neuroses—mental problems, like depression or irrational behavior—were psychological (dealing with the mind) rather than physiological (dealing with the body). To see where some of these neuroses might be coming from, Freud examined his patients' dreams. He used a technique called "free association," which therapists still use today.

Nighttime Notes

Sigmund Freud is known as "the father of dream research."

Although he is considered the father of dream research, Freud's perspective on dreams is now widely disputed. He believed that most of our dreams reflect basic human urges as well as desires from our early childhoods that we keep trying to repress—to bury, deep in our consciousness. Freud lived in very inhibited times. Today, his ideas seem out of date, particularly with their bias against women. Still, when he called dreams "the royal road to the unconscious," he became the man responsible for opening the path for all the other dream researchers who would follow him.

Carl Jung (1875–1961) was also a psychologist, born in Switzerland. Jung is probably better known today, more than forty years after his death, than he was at the height of his career. He was Freud's student, but when he developed his own theory about dreams, Jung and Freud went their separate ways. Many of Jung's discoveries about the unconscious came to him initially through dreams, which were his pathway to the deeper mysteries he studied for most of his life. His theories did a lot to redefine the new science of psychology and to make it easier for ordinary people to understand.

By studying mythology, Jung found that there were common figures—like the Hero, the Divine Child, the Wise Old Man/Old Woman, and the Shadow—that populated people's dreams all over the world, no matter what culture they came from. These dream figures, which he called "archetypes," came out of what Jung called the "collective unconscious." This is a reservoir of deep knowledge that all human beings share. Jung developed his theory of the collective unconscious from a dream he had about entering a basement.

Nighttime Notes

Jung found dream archetypes—common images that have the same meaning all over the world!

Defining the Archetypes

You can think of Jung's archetypes as universal dream figures that appear to all of us in some dreams, regardless of race, religion, or culture. When you dream of an archetype—also called archetypal images—you can usually sense that the dream is really important and that it comes from the collective unconscious. Be sure to pay close attention to dreams containing archetypal images—you never know what you may learn.

The Anima/Animus Archetype

All girls have a masculine side and boys have a feminine side that wants to be expressed from time to time. This is where the anima/animus comes in. For girls, the animus represents a hidden part of you that is male-oriented. In a dream, the animus might take the form of an incredibly wonderful boy. You might feel really close to him. The anima, meanwhile, can appear in a boy's dream as a mysterious and introspective girl.

For girls, such a dream might suggest that you can be more active and outgoing. If you are a boy, and you dream of an appealing girl who seems familiar to you, it might mean that you should take time to be more reflective and receptive, to listen to others, or to think before acting. The anima or animus might be your age, or it could be someone older than you.

Nighttime Notes

Dreaming about a unicorn means that happiness and good luck are coming into your life.

The Divine Child Archetype

The child represents innocence, growth, the power of imagination, and the sense that anything is possible. A healthy, active child appearing in a dream might represent new beginnings, a new opportunity, or a fresh start. The Child has a shadow side, as well. This is the orphan or wounded child, who represents a sense of abandonment, vulnerability, dependence, or the fear of surviving alone in the world. This form of the Divine Child might appear in dreams if you were abused or neglected in childhood. The dream might suggest that you are blaming your parents for your problems or wallowing in self-pity. Your dreaming self may be showing you that following a path of forgiveness will heal your wounds.

The Father Archetype

This is an image we all recognize. The Father is the creator, the initiator. He's all about courage, protectiveness, guidance, and a willingness to sacrifice. But you want to watch out for the shadow father. He's the dictator, who turns order and authority into control and even abuse. In dreams, the archetypal image of the Father may take the form of your actual father. It might also be any figure of authority, such as a leader or a strong guide. Dreaming of the Father might indicate the warmth and strength you get from such figures in your life, or it might show a lack of it. It all depends on what kinds of relationships you have with people who are supposed to protect and take care of you.

The Fool Archetype

As the old song goes, "Everybody plays the fool." The archetype of the Fool, or Trickster, can be a symbol for outlandish behavior that is rejected by those who conform to the accepted standards. The Fool is also an innovator who is ridiculed rather than being accepted or praised. The archetype might appear in a dream in the form of a medieval court jester. Are you breaking with conventions or following a dangerous path? This archetype might be communicating the difficulties that lie ahead if you continue playing the Fool. However, the Fool is not all bad. In breaking traditions, the Fool opens the way to new paths, new ways of thinking, and exciting innovations.

> The Fool opens the way to new paths, new ways of thinking, and exciting innovations.

The Hero Archetype

Help is on the way! The hero saves the day. The hero represents the higher path, and you can find this path when you need it, especially during an emergency. In our dreams, the archetype of the Hero reminds us that we can rise to the occasion. Dreaming of the Hero is one way we give ourselves confidence that we can do the right thing and be the good guy.

The Knight Archetype

We've seen him in the movies. The figure of the Knight represents honor and high standing, a quest for wholeness, and a desire to follow the heroic path. This archetype is associated with courtly romance and willingness to go to battle for an honorable cause. Are you searching for a knight, or are you acting like a knight? Knights are also armored, and they stand for protection.

The Mother Archetype

We all share a basic human need for comfort, nurturing, and mothering. The Mother archetype is about those human qualities that are feminine, life-giving, protecting, fruitful, and fertile. The Mother has been called the Great Mother, and in many belief systems she is the goddess of the Earth. If you dream of your birth mother, it can reflect your feelings toward her, love or guilt, admiration or fault-finding. The same would be true if you dreamed of any mother figure—someone in your life who is nurturing and comforting.

The Persona Archetype

The Persona is the face we show the world. You see this archetypal image in dreams where you remove a mask, put on makeup, or shave your face. Such dreams remind you that you are not the face that you show to the world. Your true self lies far beneath the makeup and beard. It's deeper than face value. The Persona covers and protects your true self. It allows you to present yourself in a certain way to the world.

The Wise Old Person Archetype

This archetype can be a Wise Old Man or a Wise Old Woman. It represents knowledge, strength, and understanding. In dreams, this archetype might appear in a number of forms, such as a teacher, father or mother, magician, shaman, or some other figure of authority or mystery. According to Cynthia Richmond, dream therapist and author, "When you have a dream that includes the Wise Old Man or Woman, you may be left feeling as though you had been listening to a lecture all night long. You will probably feel as though you now possess important information or understanding that you were not aware of before." The nature of that knowledge might vanish from your mind by the time you wake up, but you'll be left with the feeling that the information has been filed away for use later on.

Ancient Dreamers

In almost anything you read about dream interpretation, you'll find references to Carl Jung and Sigmund Freud. While we do consider them pioneers in dream study, they weren't the first dream experts. More than 1,800 years ago, a man named Artemidorus of Daldis wrote a dream dictionary called *The Interpretation of Dreams: Oneirocritica*. Almost two millennia later, this book is still in print and easy to find— you can find a copy on Amazon.com. That's an amazing feat, since most books go out of print within a few years of publication.

Nighttime Notes

To Artemidorus, dreams offered messages about the future. For example, if a slave dreamed of having no teeth, it meant that he would be freed. But Artemidorus also understood dreams as metaphors, which is a common way of approaching dreams today. For example, to dream of kissing someone might be a metaphor for "kiss and make up." It could also mean the "kiss of death," the end of something or, similarly, "kiss it good-bye."

Artemidorus lived in Greece around A.D. 140. It is almost certain that parts of his book are borrowed from older works, such as Assurbanipal's dream book. Assurbanipal was an Assyrian king who lived from 669–626 B.C. His book tells of the importance of dreams to both royalty and commoners. Written on clay tablets, it was found in the remnants of an ancient library at Nineveh, and it's believed to be linked to even earlier books dating all the way back to 5000 B.C.

Freud studied Artemidorus's book, but wasn't greatly influenced by it. He focused on his own idea, that dreams were related to repressed feelings. Yet Artemidorus's work has survived, and some popular dream dictionaries draw heavily on his writings. Typically, this is the kind of dream dictionary that defines most dream images in terms of good fortune or bad fortune scenarios. Most dream researchers say such dream dictionaries give us an oversimplified way of looking at dreams.

Seeing the Future in Your Dreams

Some dreams are prophetic, revealing future events. These dreams aren't very common, but maybe you can remember one. If so, write it down so that you'll have a record of it.

You might also ask friends and family members if they remember any dreams that came true and jot them down below. For instance, a friend of mine told me of a dream he had where his family's cabin tilted sideways, then collapsed. It could have been symbolic, maybe related to some part of his life that seemed to be falling apart. But this time that wasn't the case. My friend actually went out and checked along the foundation of his cabin. He found that two concrete blocks in one corner had slipped. The cabin really was in danger of tilting and even slipping off its foundation, if he had allowed it to remain that way.

Birds

The appearance of a bird could relate to a wish for freedom, to fly away. A caged bird represents a feeling of being trapped. Birds can also be spiritual symbols. Among certain Native American tribes, an eagle symbolizes spiritual knowledge.

Three

Tracking Your Dreams

I was not looking from my dreams to interpret my life, but rather my life to interpret my dreams.

—SUSAN SONTAG, *THE BENEFACTOR*

My thirteen-year-old daughter didn't want to wake up. "Let me sleep fifteen minutes more. I'm having a good dream."

I was tempted to ask Megan to tell me the dream, but I let her sleep. She woke up on her own ten minutes later. Another ten minutes passed before I saw her.

"So what was your dream?"

She stared at me, a sleepy look still on her face. "What are you talking about?"

"You said you were having a good dream when I woke you up."

She made a face as if she'd just been handed a surprise math test. "I did? I don't remember that."

Neurologists, those scientists who study the brain, have proven that everybody dreams. But some people have such a hard time remembering even traces of their dreams that it *seems* to them that they don't dream at all. Dreams are like that sometimes: here one moment, gone the next. Still, whether they remember or not, everyone dreams.

As you begin to learn more about your dreams, you can think of them like your own personal movies that run every night. Crawl into bed, close your eyes, and wait for the drama to unfold.

Anyone can track their dreams—you just have to make a little effort. You can start by programming yourself to dream and to remember what you dream. It's easier than it sounds. Before you fall asleep, simply tell yourself several times that you'll remember your dreams long enough to jot down the details when you wake up. The best time to make this suggestion is right as you're starting to fall asleep. That's when your mind is most likely to follow your inner command.

Nighttime Notes

Keep a notebook by your bed so you can record your dreams as they happen.

Imagine that you're taking a dream camera to bed with you. Imagine you're taking dream snapshots during the night. When you wake up, either during the night or in the morning, you'll have these snapshots as memories of what you dreamed about.

It may sound weird, but it works. When you first wake up, you may not recall any dreams. But after a few seconds, it's as if a veil is lifted. The dreams reveal themselves. If you're having trouble, you can trigger your memory by returning to your favorite position for sleeping. Just relax and ask for your dreams. After a few moments, roll over to your other side.

Start out slowly by telling yourself to remember the most important dream of the night. If that works, then tell yourself that you'll remember all of your dreams. Often times, you remember the last one first. You can work backward from there. As you recall the previous dream in the night's sequence, it triggers memories of the one that came before it.

Recording Your Dreams

Try to write down your dream as soon as you wake up and before you forget it, which probably won't be long. Keep a notepad and pen by your bed and maybe a little flashlight or penlight in case you wake up after a dream during the night. Without thinking too much about it, jot down as much as you can remember.

At first, your scrawls may be nearly indecipherable, but with practice you can improve your writing so that you'll be able to easily transcribe your notes in the morning. The important thing is being able to read what you wrote in the morning. Alternately, you can use a recorder to tape your recollection of the dream when you wake up.

Tips for Remembering Dreams
Take a look at these great tips to help you remember your dreams:

- As you go to sleep, give yourself a suggestion to remember your dreams.
- Keep a pen and pad and a small flashlight at your bedside.
- Don't be judgmental about your dreams.
- Don't censor yourself.
- Don't trivialize your dreams.
- Go back to your last sleeping position to see if it triggers your memory. Then roll over.
- Try to wake up without an alarm.

Don't worry if your dream doesn't make sense. In the dream world, things don't always happen in a linear and logical way. You can disappear and reappear somewhere else. You can walk on the ceiling or fly through the air. No problem. You might even find yourself telling your little brother or sister how much you love him or her, even though in your waking life the little twerp drives you crazy.

Nighttime Notes

Don't question the value of your dream. Maybe it seems silly. So what? Just write it down! What seems like nonsense later may turn out to make a lot of sense.

Sometimes dreams are so vivid that you wake up during the night and think that you'll *definitely* remember this one. But by morning, all you can remember is how the dream made you feel—and of course how sure you were you'd remember it. The best way to recall your dreams is to record them as soon as they're finished. If you wake up during the night with a dream on your mind, don't even wait until morning. Write it down immediately.

Just the act of recording your dreams helps you remember them. At first, you may be able to recall only scraps of your last dream before waking, but by writing down the fragment you may recall more details. With practice you'll be able to recall more details of each dream and remember more dreams, too. Eventually, the process becomes automatic, as familiar as the morning ritual of brushing your teeth.

With this method, you soon may start remembering as many as four or five dreams on a good night. Scribble down the main points of your dreams, then first thing in the morning expand on your notes in your journal.

For two weeks, make suggestions to yourself to remember your dreams. If you still have trouble after that, you might try a more drastic method.

* Set your alarm for an early hour, say four in the morning. (During the school year, do this on the weekend.) While alarms can distract you and make it harder to recall your dreams, they also can trigger the memory of your most recent dream.

* When you wake up, ask yourself what you were dreaming, then immediately record anything that comes to mind.
* Only use the alarm method if you're having problems waking up on your own. Before resorting to the alarm, as you fall asleep, tell yourself you'll wake up at a certain time.
* It won't be long before you're awakening within five or ten minutes of your target time.

As you are recording your dreams, try to avoid thinking that you'll remember them later and record them when you have more time or you're more awake. Dream memories are fleeting and elusive. As time goes by, remembering a dream becomes more and more like trying to catch a fluttering butterfly without a net. After an hour or two, probably the only thing you'll remember is that you were going to record a dream.

Remember, no matter how confusing, meaningless, or embarrassing your dreams may be, don't trivialize them. What seems trivial now could turn out to be significant and not embarrassing at all.

> *Either we have no dreams or we have interesting ones*
> *—we need to learn to be awake in the same way.*
> —FRIEDRICH NIETZSCHE

Creating Your Dream Journal

After you've recorded your dreams, the next step is to use your rough notes to create a dream journal. Your journal should reflect your personality. You might choose a spiral notebook for your journal or, better yet, a blank cloth-bound book. Make it personal by decorating it

with a decorative design or stickers. Or you can give it a title, like "Dream On," "The Dream World," or "Dream Weavings." Be creative.

Nighttime Notes

When you set aside the time to create a journal that's personal and expressive, you're sending a strong message to your inner self. You're saying that you take your dreams seriously and that you want to remember them and work with them.

Make the Most of Your Dream Journal

Once you've personalized your dream journal, it's time to put it to work. The tips below will help you begin the exciting journey into your dreams.

- Always give each dream its own title, such as "Cat in the Basement."
- When you describe a dream, describe the characters and events. Write down the most striking thing about your dream.
- Include as many details as possible—colors, shapes, action, dialogue, or whatever else stands out.

As you work with your dream journal, you'll start building a record of your dream life. You'll be able to recognize repeating dream themes and look back on your dreams and learn from them.

Here's an example of some rough dream notes, followed by a sample entry into a dream journal. You can see how the details of the dream are revealed when the notes are expanded in the journal entry.

Notes: 10/17

Phantom, winning Kentucky Derby. Mom and Kyle in stands, Cait competing. Phantom racing down backstretch. Then suddenly at American Horse Show, jumping, gold cup and medal. Cait and her horse Gary win dressage.

Ride to Glory

I dreamed that my horse, Phantom, and I won the Kentucky Derby and the American Horse Show. Pretty good, even for a dream! My mom and Kyle are in the stands watching. Cait F. is competing in a dressage competition on her big Fresian named Gary.

The starting bell rings and Phantom leaps out of the starting gate and into the lead of the Kentucky Derby. I can even hear the announcer saying, "And they're off . . ."

I'm steering Phantom along the track and saving his speed so he will have more left in the end. I'm wearing purple and teal racing silks—my favorite colors. Phantom is running his heart out as we pound down the backstretch of the Churchill Downs racetrack. I ask Phantom for a little more power and we win the Kentucky Derby by six lengths!

I feel Phantom jump and we're suddenly competing in a jumper class at the American Horse Show in New York. I'm wearing pure white breeches, gleaming black tall boots, and a pink hunter jacket. We make a clear round with no faults and the fastest time, so we win. People run up to congratulate me. Phantom is draped in roses and I'm handed a gold cup and a gold medal. Cait rides over on Gary and stands next to me and Phantom for the winners' photo. She's handed a gold cup and a medal, too, for winning the dressage competition.

Sometimes the meaning of your dreams is obvious as soon as you write them in your journal. The act of writing down the details may give you enough time to think about it and understand it. However, many of your dreams may puzzle you. So, in the next chapter, we'll take a look at how to interpret dreams, especially those difficult ones that don't seem to make any sense—at least not right away.

Keys to Recalling Your Dreams

Here's a list of things to look for in recalling dreams. Remember that these are just guidelines. Some of the questions will apply to your dreams, and some may not. You can jot this exercise in your dream journal.

1. Name your dream.
2. Write a one-sentence summary of your dream, noting the most striking image, which is probably related to the title.
3. Look for answers to the reporter's questions—who, what, when, where, and how.
   - Who was with you? Friends, family, strangers?
   - What were you doing in the dream? What were others doing? What did you or others say?
   - When was it? Day or night? Was it dark or light?
   - Where were you? Describe the scene, including the colors, the shapes, whatever stands out.
   - How did the dream feel? Familiar, odd, pleasant, upsetting?
4. Note how you felt when you woke up. Were you rested, exhilarated, afraid, sad, happy?
5. Does the dream remind you of anything that took place during the previous day? Does it connect to something from the past?

Horse

A horse symbolizes strength, power, endurance, majesty, and virility. A boy dreaming of a horse might desire manhood; a woman might be expressing a desire for intimacy. Riding a horse suggests one is in a powerful position.

Four

Interpreting Your Dreams

The dream is a little hidden door in the innermost and most secret recesses of the soul, opening into that cosmic night.
—Carl Jung

So let's say that you're now able to remember your dreams, and you're beginning to jot them down. You're noting how you feel about them and whether they remind you of anything that took place during the previous day. But what do they mean, and how do you interpret them?

Look It Up

Dream dictionaries and glossaries—like the one at the back of this book—can be helpful in providing clues and the symbolic meaning of images. However, you can't rely on them to interpret your dreams. Most of the time, there is more than one possible explanation of a dream image. It's up to you to decide which one, if any, makes the most sense. There are times when your dreams are going to be too personal, and the standard meanings just don't fit. For example, no dictionary is going to tell you what it means for you to dream about a friend from third grade who moved away years ago. But you may know exactly what that person means to you.

Nighttime Notes

Your dreams are totally your own—there may not always be a book explanation, so look deep into yourself to find the meaning.

Hunt for Hidden Clues

Keep in mind that dreams often have many layers of meaning. Sometimes the most obvious meaning is not the only one. Say you

> Keep in mind that dreams often have many layers of meaning. Sometimes the most obvious meaning is not the only one.

dream that the fence on the border of your yard suddenly falls down. What are fences to you? They enclose and protect something. They define the edge or boundary.

So what does it mean in a dream when your fence collapses? Maybe the fence around your house in your waking life really is falling down. On another level, a falling fence could mean that you've lost some kind of protection. It could also mean that the barriers that hold you back are falling, that you are ready to expand beyond the current boundaries in your life and move into something new.

It's even possible that all of those interpretations are correct! On an everyday level, a fence might need repair. But the dream image could also be a symbol for personal barriers that might be falling. That's what happens when you go beyond your comfort zone and take a chance on something new. You lose the protection you used to get just from staying within those secure—but limiting—boundaries.

Keys to Unlocking Your Dreams

Dream dictionaries may provide you with some good, general clues for beginning to understand your dreams, but what if you're looking for a little more? This chapter can help you go deeper.

> *Last night I dreamed I ate a ten-pound marshmallow, and when I woke up, my pillow was gone.*
> —TOMMY COOPER

Connect Your Dream to Your Waking Life

If you spent hours at the mall yesterday, and you dream of hanging out at the mall, you might simply be processing the day's events. Likewise, if you were focused intensely on some activity, such as a major homework project, you might have a dream related to it. But, remember, dreams can have many layers, and even processing dreams about daily events can have a deeper meaning. Take this dream, which was recorded by a fourteen-year-old girl.

> *"I was arguing with my mother, just like I'd done after dinner and felt frustrated because she wouldn't let me go out with my friends. I went to bed angry with the matter still up in the air. But in the dream, I ran outside and suddenly I was walking with two girls in a park near my house. I didn't know them, but somehow I knew they had powers and I wanted to be like them.*
>
> *"We heard barking and growling and I saw a vicious dog leaping up and snapping at the legs of two little kids who were trapped on the jungle gym. One of the girls told me to use my powers to stop the dog. So I started yelling at the dog and it floated into the air and away from the children. It was still growling and angry, but the kids managed to get away."*

How would you interpret this dream? A generic interpretation would be that the girl wants to obtain power in her life so she can help others. Maybe so, but that's only scratching the surface. Look a little deeper at what happened during her day, namely, the argument with her mother. In her waking life, nothing was resolved, and she went to bed with the matter "still up in the air," in her own words. Dogs often symbolize instinct or raw emotion. With

> Dogs often symbolize instinct or raw emotion.

this in mind, we could say that the dream might relate to the girl's attempt to control her emotions, which are symbolized by the angry dog floating in the air.

Finding connections between your dreams and the events in your waking life is a great way to try to understand what's going on inside of you. Let's say before going to bed you watched a scary movie in which someone was being chased. If later on that night you had a dream in which *you* were being chased, it would be fair to say that you might just be processing the

Nighttime Notes

Listen up! Your unconscious mind might be trying to give you an important message about your life.

day's events in your dream. On the other hand, your unconscious mind might choose to use the movie scene as a way to send you a message. Are you running away from something in your life? Who's chasing you? If it's someone you know, what does that person mean to you? If it's a stranger or a monster, what do you think the figure could represent? Of course, you need to look at the other elements in the dream, too. Ultimately, it's up to you to decide what your dreams mean in relation to your life.

Look for Metaphors and Puns

You might already know that metaphors and puns are forms of wordplay. Think of both metaphors and puns as words that are "used wrong" to make a point. For example, take an *angry* sunburn. Sunburns don't actually have emotions, of course, but if you've ever had a bad one, you know the description's not far off. That's a metaphor. A pun is a humorous play on words which suggests a different meaning. Like the guy who spotted the Dalmatian. Or the racehorse who was on track to win. Get it?

Your dreaming self, that secret part of you that uses dreams to send messages, likes to use metaphors and puns to make its point. It's a good idea to look for symbols that could be metaphorical or part of a pun.

Pardon the Pun

Your dreams may be trying to tell you something through pun or metaphor.

Fun Puns:

Dream: A package arrives in the mail

Meaning: A male may enter your life soon

Dream: Your girlfriend hands you a letter

Meaning: There's something you need to let her do

Dream: You're riding on a train

Meaning: You're in training for something

Dream: You pick up a needle, or try to pick it up

Meaning: Are you looking for a needle in a haystack? Or, is someone "needling" you?

Meaningful Metaphors

Dream: A snake slithering toward you

Meaning: Is there a "snake in the grass" or a deceitful person in your life?

Dream: You are taking an awful-tasting spoonful of cough syrup

Meaning: You are suffering the consequences of something, or "getting a taste of your own medicine"

Remember, dreams can have more than one meaning. The correct meaning is the one that feels right, so it's up to you to decide which interpretations are right for you. Look for the symbols, especially the ones that repeat themselves, and make your interpretation. If you get stuck, just turn to the dream dictionary in the back of this book for help.

My Personal Dream Dictionary

You can create your own custom dream dictionary in the back of your dream journal. All you have to do is jot down the symbols that appear in the dreams you've recorded. Pay careful attention to the puns or metaphors in your dreams that can be connected to your waking life. If there is more than one possible interpretation, choose the one that best fits you and your situation.

Follow Your Feelings

The way you feel about a dream might be as significant as its contents. That's why it's important when you write down your dream that you record your feelings. For example, your feelings about the other characters in your dream may help to determine its meaning. Likewise, if you're doing something really weird, like vomiting up green liquid or sinking like a rock to the bottom of a pool, the way you feel about it is key.

Consider the following dream, recorded by fifteen-year-old Melissa.

> In my dream, I was at home when this older girl I don't know comes to my door. She's into the gothic look with black lips and black clothes. I immediately know that she's a witch. I see

45

another girl with her who's also into witchcraft. As if to confirm my thoughts, she disappears and reappears. They want me to go with them. I feel good about it. I want to be just like them.

There are lots of possibilities for what Melissa's dream means. Guess which of the two possibilities below she chose for herself.

1. Melissa could be in danger of making a bad decision.
2. Melissa is yearning for more, independence and power.

The second meaning is the closest to Melissa's true feelings. She mentioned that she felt good about going with the girls. She knew they meant her no harm. By paying attention to her feelings, Melissa was able to understand her dream as her desire to find herself and her own sense of power.

Watch for Warning Signs

Many of our dreams are psychological in nature; that is, they bring junk from our subconscious minds up to the surface. But every now and then you may get a warning in a dream that's directly related to your daily life. It's a good idea to look at every dream as though it just might relate to something that is coming in your future.

For instance, this dream was reported by seventeen-year-old Jerry, whose parents had separated several weeks earlier. His father, possibly feeling guilty, had bought Jerry his first car, a ten-year-old Mustang, a few weeks earlier.

I was driving my car through a strange area. A lot of the trees looked black and the ground was blackened like there'd been a forest fire here. I could even smell the burnt wood. Suddenly, my car started shaking. I gripped the steering wheel and then I heard an explosion. The car swerved just like it would do with a blowout. Then I hit something and it flipped over. I crawled out the window. But I was stuck on the side of the road in the burned-out forest and it was getting dark. I noticed one green plant poking up through the black landscape and I couldn't take my eyes off it. That's when I woke up in a sweat. I was really relieved that it was a dream.

If you look at the events in the dream as symbols of what was happening in his life, the dream suggests that Jerry felt "sidelined." His life had been turned upside down. He wasn't able to move ahead. But in this case, Jerry also considered the literal meaning of the dream. He took a look at his car and discovered a gash in his left rear tire that could have caused a blowout. The dream alerted him to a problem he didn't know about. By keeping alert and taking action, Jerry succeeded in keeping the dream from coming true. In that way, this was a *precognitive* dream.

But the symbolic meaning was just as true as the literal meaning of the dream. He did feel that his life had been turned upside down and that a forest fire had swept through his world. But the single green plant indicated that things were starting to get better.

It's always a good idea to look for such warnings in your dreams, as long as you don't start to obsess over them. As you remember from Chapter 1, in ancient times, most dreams were thought to be precognitive or prophetic, as signs of good luck or bad luck. But today researchers believe dreams are largely symbolic.

In other words, if you dream that you died, the good news is that it doesn't mean you're about to drop dead. Instead, it probably relates to the death of an old part of you. For example, if you switch schools or you're getting ready to graduate from middle school to high school, these changes could trigger a dream about your death. You have changed, and you've moved ahead into your new life. In such a case, death would not be a loss, but a natural part of growing up. (See Chapter 7 for more on dreams of death.)

Monitor Your Dreaming Self

Pay attention to yourself in your dreams. You're always there, after all, either as one of the characters or as an observer. Some dream researchers even say that all of the characters in your dreams are you, in one form or another. Usually, though, you have a sense of yourself as the central figure.

Note how you act in your dreams.

* Do you flee from challenges or confront them?
* Do you tend to watch what's going on, or do you jump into the action?
* Are you older and more mature, or are you younger and smaller?
* Do you make choices, or do the other characters in your dream make the decisions?

Robert Moss, author of *Conscious Dreaming,* suggests monitoring your dreaming self over several dreams. Seeing how you act helps you to interpret the deeper meanings of your dreams and will help you deal with daily problems. Moss states, "You will find that you will become more observant of the contents of your mind in waking life, and more conscious of how your attitudes shape the reality you think you inhabit."

When you follow yourself in a dream, you realize that you can make dramatic personal changes. Take the following dream, recorded by twelve-year-old Heather.

> *I'm surprised to find that I'm a full grown woman, but I'm still in seventh grade. I'm the only adult in the class besides the teacher, but nobody seems to notice. It's all boring stuff, baby stuff to me. Then suddenly I'm no longer in class. Now I'm at a restaurant with my mom and dad and I'm my regular self. They're talking about politics and other adult stuff. I'm half-listening, but I'm bored again. I'd rather be playing with my friends.*

Heather often finds school work boring. So when she appeared in an adult body in class, it reflected her feeling of being older than her age. But with her parents she's a child again. Even though they're talking about adult matters, she still feels like a child. So paying attention to images of herself in the dream was the key to understanding it.

Hunting My Dreaming Self

Take a look at the last dream that you recorded, and see if you can answer these questions. Your answers will probably vary from dream to dream, but a pattern may emerge if you track several dreams.

- What do you look like? Are you the same as your waking life? If not, how are you different?
- Are you present and involved or just observing?
- Do you take an active role in the action, or are you just going along with events? Do you interact with others or watch them?
- Are you acting the same as you do during your waking life or different?

Interview the Dream Characters

A fun way to interpret your dreams is to interview the characters and ask them what they're doing in your dream. It's surprising what you can find out by this method. There are a couple of different ways you can do these interviews. The important point is to allow your imagination to run wild. Don't hold back.

Make sure the dream is fresh in your mind. Hopefully, you've described it in your dream journal, and you're ready to work with the characters. Read over your entry and think about what you want to find out. What bothers you about the dream? Which of the characters are you concerned about?

Set up two chairs so that they face each other. Sit down in one and imagine one of the dream characters seated across from you. Remember that it doesn't have to be a human. If a dragon was chasing you, breathing fire down your neck, picture it seated across from you waiting for the interview to begin. Ask your question. For example, you might want to know why the dragon was chasing you.

Then switch places. Take the dragon's chair. Imagine that you're the fire-breathing creature and it's time to answer the question. Say whatever comes to mind. Then switch places again. You might jot down the answer and ask another question. Keep going until you're satisfied you've gotten all the answers. If you can't think of a question, just ask the dream character, "Why are you in my dream? What are you telling me?"

If you can't think of a question, just ask the dream character, "Why are you in my dream? What are you telling me?"

If you're uncomfortable using the chairs, you can carry out the interview through your dream journal. Write down your question, addressing the dream character. Then jot down whatever comes to mind. This method is less complicated than switching chairs back and forth, but it might be harder to get answers, especially if this is your first time interviewing a dream character.

Here's an example of a dream and the ensuing interview. In this case, sixteen-year-old Teri used the chair method to get her answers.

Dead Man Walking

Three weeks ago, I broke up with my boyfriend, Todd, after he told me he wants to be freer. I'm still trying to get over it, and I hate it when I run into him in the hall at school. It reminds me of how things used to be. I know that's over, but part of me keeps hoping things will change.

In the dream, someone told me that Todd was killed in a car accident. I'm surprised but not sad or shocked, like I would be in waking life. Then I'm outside at night and there's Todd. He's all bloody and I know he's dead. But he's walking right toward me. He acts like he doesn't see me, but I run. Everywhere I go after that, I see him, even though no one else seems to notice him. He's always walking toward me. Finally, I scream at him to go away. "You're dead!"

That's when I woke up shaking and sweating. I was really glad it was a dream.

The Interview

I imagine that Todd is sitting across from me. He looks like he did in the dream.

"Okay, what are you trying to tell me?"

"I'm dead."

"If you're dead, why do you keep walking toward me everywhere I go?"

"Because you don't really believe I'm dead. You think I'm going to come alive again."

51

"Are you?"

"I'm dead. It's over. If you accept that, you won't see me all the time."

At that point, I stop the interview. It's all too clear. I've got to stop thinking about Todd and just let it go. After all, he doesn't want to be with me, and he's certainly not the only guy in the world.

Even though Teri was puzzled by the dream of her old boyfriend, it didn't take long for her to understand it once she sat down and began interviewing the grotesque dream-Todd. The message was clear. The relationship was over, and it was time for her to move on.

In the next two chapters, you'll learn even more ways to deal with your dreams. Think of dreams as multilayered mysteries that play nightly on your own private inner theater. The deeper you dig, the more you discover.

Monster

Often associated with nightmares, a frightening being or beast often indicates that you are afraid of facing something within you that needs to change. Also an internal conflict or, especially for a child, fear of changes or new elements in one's environment, the need to grow and change.

Five

Cooking Your Dreams

Take, if you must, this little bag of dreams,
Unloose the cord, and they will wrap you
round.

————WILLIAM BUTLER YEATS

Imagine what it would be like to be able to go to bed, plan what dreams you wanted to have, and then go to sleep and have those dreams. If that sounds impossible to you, think again. As you get better at remembering, recording, and interpreting your dreams, there are ways you can improve and advance your dreaming skills.

It is actually possible to "incubate" dreams, that is, to program yourself to have dreams that will guide you in specific areas of your life. In addition, you can learn how to re-enter a dream, repeat it, and even alter its ending. It's sort of like cooking up your own dreams—it *really* works!

Let's start by looking at how you can request a dream.

Dream Incubation

Dream incubation was practiced in ancient times in Mesopotamia, Egypt, Greece, and Rome. People actually traveled to temples dedicated to specific gods, where they spent the night in hopes of receiving a dream that would heal, illuminate, or resolve a problem.

In Egypt, those seeking a dream sometimes spent the night in a cave and performed a magic ritual. They used a special lamp with magic words and figures inscribed on it. The individual would gaze into the flame until a vision of a god appeared. The person then went to sleep, and the god appeared in a dream to provide guidance.

Today, however, you don't need to travel far to incubate a dream. You can do it right at home.

Nighttime Notes

The first step in dream incubation is knowing what to ask for. Are you concerned about a relationship, a health problem, a disruption in your daily life? Whatever it is, you can request a dream *and* get an answer.

Write down your question in your dream journal before you go to bed. This ritual helps fortify the question in your mind as you go to sleep. Then repeat the question to yourself a few times as you start to doze off. Of course you also need to follow the steps for recalling and interpreting your dream in the morning.

The following cool dream was programmed by Caitlin, a fourteen-year-old, who requested a dream about horseback riding, her favorite activity.

I saw my backyard and it was about five times larger than it is in real life. What was odd was that I couldn't smell the grass, hear the birds, or feel the wind. I stepped onto a wood mounting block used for climbing onto a horse. I smiled as I looked around and climbed onto a blue mountain bike that was probably five feet tall, as tall as a horse. The bike glided around my yard at an amazingly fast speed. I didn't even have to pedal. It was as if I was riding a horse.

Suddenly, the bike morphed into Tempo, the huge bay thoroughbred mare who I absolutely love to ride in real life. I didn't seem to notice the bike had changed. I just saw myself laugh gleefully and kept Tempo cantering with her long, smooth stride around my yard. It was even more fun with my stirrups real short, making me sit like a jockey.

The dream ended as I turned a corner like a barrel racer on Tempo and my alarm went off. I kept my eyes closed and lay in bed, going through the dream and re-experiencing the feelings. I remember feeling happy, relaxed, and worry-free, just like I do when I really ride. I felt well rested and exhilarated. The dream was really joyful and I was amazed that the incubation actually had worked.

Finding Your Question

Here's a series of easy steps you can take to help you identify the areas of your life that you might like to change with the help of your dreams.

- Take the practice of dream incubation seriously. That means you want to avoid silly or trivial questions. When you are ready to make your request, imagine that you have entered a dream temple. Keep in mind that the ancients journeyed to the dream temples when a serious matter needed to be resolved.

- Make sure that you are completely open to getting your question answered. Be aware that your dreaming self will provide the truth, even if you don't like the answer.

- Make your question simple and direct, but don't ask a yes or no question. For example, if you are going to be moving to Asheville, North Carolina, instead of asking if you're going to like the city, ask *how* you will like it.

- Avoid ambiguous questions. For example, don't ask questions that pose choices, because it might be unclear which of the choices your dream is telling you about. If you want to know,

"Am I better off going out with Bill or Ron?" phrase the question more directly, such as, "How would I get along with Bill?"

- You can also ask broad questions, rather than specific ones. For example, you might ask any of the following:
  - "How can I improve my life?"
  - "What path should I follow?"
  - "Why do I feel this way?"
  - "What am I doing wrong?"

When you write down your question in your dream journal, you'll have a chance to think more about it and maybe revise the wording.

It's a good idea to incubate a dream on a quiet night when you have time and you're not excited from an evening out with friends. That way you can spend some time in preparation. You might light a candle or turn on some soft music as you prepare your question. Likewise, it's best if you have time in the morning to really think about your interpretation of the dream. Take time to consider it, and see how the dream and your understanding of it fits into your life.

Nighttime Notes

With practice, chances are good that you will soon begin receiving answers to your questions from your dreaming self. Remember, though, dream incubation isn't a game.

If your dream doesn't seem to answer your question, don't worry about it. Let it rest. Sometimes, after a few minutes or even an hour or two, the connection suddenly pops into your head, giving you sudden illumination—sort of like one of those light bulbs you see over cartoon characters' heads. If you're still stumped, try again. If you continue having difficulty, look closely at your question. Do you really want an answer? If so, maybe you can rephrase it to make it clearer. The best time to begin your practice is when you have a question or concern that truly matters to you. Most likely, that's when your desire for knowledge will incubate and bear fruit, in the form of a dream with a message.

Dream Re-Entry

Imagine that while you were in a dream, you found a doorway that let you escape and re-enter your dream at any time. That's what the process of dream re-entry is all about. The easiest way of returning to a dream is to do it right away, while you're still sleepy and the memory of the inner drama is fresh.

Nighttime Notes

When you wake up from a recent dream, dream re-entry lets you go back into it to clarify the things that happened. Famous psychologist Carl Jung called it "dreaming the dream onward."

Dream researcher Robert Moss believes that dream re-entry is the best way of dealing with nightmares. It allows you to go back into the dream and alter the results by confronting whatever terrified you. Moss points out that dream re-entry requires two things: "your ability to focus clearly on a remembered scene from your dream, and your ability to relax and allow your consciousness to flow back inside that scene."

Tips on Dream Re-Entry

- The easiest way to find your way back into a dream is to focus on the location. What do you remember about your dream's

scenery? You don't need much detail. Even a single view of a building, a room, a street, or a landmark will do.

- Before you re-enter, make sure you're prepared. Know the main thing you want to find out about the dream. Write down your question, and keep it simple. It might be specific about the meaning of some incident or character in the dream. For example, if you're being chased, you can turn on the stalker and ask: "Why are you chasing me?" Your question also could be general, such as: "What is this dream telling me?"

- Think about the details of your dream, especially the parts that stood out the most. Was there a particular character who caught your attention? If so, you might pose your question to him or her. You can also ask yourself who is the best character in the dream to answer the question.

- Relax and breathe deeply, allowing yourself to return to the dream state. Focus on the location. Count backward from ten or twenty as you focus on the location. Once you are there, look around for details that you might have missed the first time.

- Follow the action. See if anything has changed. For example, you might notice that now new characters have entered the dream. Let it unwind beyond the point where it stopped last time.

- Enter a conversation with one of the characters. Ask your question. Be prepared for an answer that might come in some form other than what you expect. You might even get an answer to another question that's more important.

- Take your answer back with you and quickly jot down the details of everything you remember. Note if your question was answered, and carefully consider the meaning of any answer you got.

Dream re-entry is an advanced technique, so don't expect immediate results. The first time you try it, you might drift off into another dream. Alternately, you might drift back into your dream but lose your conscious awareness. In that case, you probably won't ask your question. Even so, when you wake up, you might have an answer if you can recall the dream.

Dream incubation and re-entry is a great way to get to know your dreams and even influence them. You can also expand your understanding of dreams when you share them with others. That's what the next chapter is all about.

Oak

An oak tree, a sacred symbol in Celtic lore, represents strength, stability, endurance, truth, and wisdom. A dream with an oak may suggest that a strong, proper foundation has been established in a matter.

60

Six

Dream Sharing

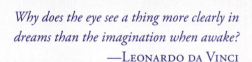

*Why does the eye see a thing more clearly in
dreams than the imagination when awake?*
—LEONARDO DA VINCI

One of the most frequently told stories in the world of dream research is a fascinating tale about a culture whose people shared their dreams with each other every day and even governed themselves through dreaming. They are the Senoi, a forest people who still reside in the mountains of Malaysia. Each day began with members of the family, including children, sharing their dreams from the previous night. Family members were asked about their behavior in their dreams, and suggestions were given for correcting behavior and attitude in future dreams.

Nighttime Notes

According to a researcher in the 1930s, the Senoi used dreams as a powerful tool for holding their society together.

Once the dream-sharing by families was finished, the village council met, and the serious dream work began. The members discussed the symbols in each reported dream to determine their meaning. Then they would act upon the dreams. For example, if it was thought that a dream meant the tribe should build a new community building, those who agreed on the meaning might adopt it as a project.

More recent scholars visiting the Senoi say that dream work no longer plays a large role in the tribe. As a result, some skeptics have questioned whether it ever really did. However, as dream researcher

Jeremy Taylor points out, the Senoi approach to dealing with dreams, especially the nightmarish ones that we'll discuss in Chapter 9, actually works. And that's what really matters.

The Senoi didn't criticize or condemn any actions that took place in a person's dream. Instead, they suggested alternative behaviors and actions. Anything negative about the dream was transformed into something positive. Fear was changed into courage, danger was avoided, and pleasure and a positive outcome were achieved. These dream actions were then carried out, in one form or another, in waking life. For instance, if someone dreamed that he was hostile toward another person in the tribe, after that dream he would go out of his way to be friendly. Imagine if the leaders of warring nations took such an approach based on dreams!

Nighttime Notes

You can take the idea of dream sharing and make it part of your own dream work. Dream sharing is a valuable tool for helping yourself and others.

But let's stay focused on our own lives. It's usually easier to see things in other people's dreams that they might overlook. Likewise, they may see meaning in your dreams that you've missed. So as your dream work advances, you might begin discussing dreams with your friends.

Getting Started

If you would like to try the method that the Senoi used, you can start your very own dream group. Dream work takes focus and concentration, and it pays to be consistent. The members of your group should be willing to commit to a series of sessions.

Nighttime Notes

The easiest way to start a dream group is to keep things small. Include just one or two other people, preferably friends who live close by and who are also interested in their dreams.

Once you get your dream group together, plan to meet just once a week for six weeks. If you start out meeting more than that, you may find that you don't have enough dreams to discuss. But if you leave too much time between meetings, your group might lose interest.

As you work with your dreams, word might spread about what you're doing. Almost everyone wonders about what their dreams mean, and people are going to be interested in your group. So you might find your group growing. You are all on the same journey, all sharing your dream experiences. Even if you haven't always gotten along all that well with someone in the group, the barriers between you and that person will soon break down. Dream sharing is powerful.

You also need to consider who's going to take the lead and work as a guide and organizer. If you're the one forming the group, it might be you, especially if you've been working with your dreams for a while. But if there's a natural leader who seems to have abilities working with others in a sensitive and compassionate manner, you might step aside after your initial effort to get everyone together. You can also take turns as guide for the day, so everyone has a chance to lead. That's a good way to avoid friction and competition among members.

Nighttime Notes

When it comes to your dreams, you are the "expert." The others are your assistants.

Whoever takes the lead, though, needs to understand that dream work is democratic. No one person has all the answers.

Guidelines for Your Dream Group

1. The single most important thing in working with a dream group is mutual trust. Everyone in the group must be willing to share their dreams. If you're allowing others into your dreams, they must allow you to enter their inner world as well.

2. You are the final authority on the meaning of your dream.

3. You cannot tell anyone else what his or her dream is about. You can only tell them what it would mean to you if it were your dream. That's why you should preface any comment about someone else's dream with the phrase, "If it were my dream . . ."

4. Sharing dreams does not mean giving up your right to privacy. You don't have to tell someone about a personal matter related to your dream if you're uncomfortable about it. Likewise, you shouldn't try to pry too deeply into someone else's life if they don't willingly volunteer personal details.

5. Dreams told within the group shouldn't be revealed to anyone outside the group without the dreamer's permission.

Choose a place to meet where your group will have privacy. The fewer distractions the better. For example, a room that you can close off from the rest of the house works better than a family room in the center of activity. You don't want curious, but annoying, little brothers and sisters intruding, unless they are old enough to join the group. As noted above, you only want active participants.

Once you've decided upon a place to meet, for example, at your house after school on Friday or on Sunday afternoon, try to keep that the regular time. For a few days before your meeting, pay particularly close attention to your dreams. If you're not having any that you can remember, ask for a dream that you will remember before going to bed. As always, make sure you write it down in your dream journal as soon as possible.

Your Dream Group

Okay. So you're at your first dream group meeting, and you're all prepared with a dream. Now what? It's important to take this gathering seriously, whether there are just two of you or seven or eight. You or someone else should serve as the dream guide, the one who takes charge of the meeting and keeps things focused.

Light a candle, and gather in a circle around it. Take a few moments just to be quiet together. You might want to spend this time thinking about your dreams, or you might use it to get centered and relaxed, taking in slow, deep breaths. Quiet down your mind. Let go of everything else but your interest in dreams.

The dream guide might break the silence by reciting a short affirmation. For example, you might say something like this:

Here we gather our energies together
As we open our dreams
To wisdom and understanding
As we remember who we are
And learn who we are becoming.

At this point, each of you should state your name, then the name of your dream. Since strange things happen in dreams, the names can be strange, too. For example, when seventeen-year-old Julie attended a dream group that was meeting for the first time, she called one of her dreams "Clown Turns into Umbrella." The name was strange and intriguing, and she remembered that everyone was curious.

The dream group works when all those present are active and participating. You might find sometimes, especially with new members, that someone will claim not to remember any dreams or that they're just here "to watch." Without being confrontational, the dream guide should take charge of the situation. Everyone in the group has to understand that the meetings are about dream *work*, not dream *watch*. A good way to tackle this is to be kind but firm. You might say, "Okay, you get one free pass. Next time you'll have to pay, just like the rest of us. The entry fee is one dream."

Now it's time to take turns sharing dreams. Robert Moss suggests telling your dream in the present tense as if it's happening right now. Julie's dream, "Clown Turns into Umbrella," would start out like this: "A clown leaps out of the bushes and charges toward me" (instead of "leaped" and "charged"). While you certainly can bring notes, try to avoid reading your dream. Speak slowly, and turn your dream into a dramatic story, if possible.

In Julie's dream, the charging clown did a cartwheel, then magically turned into an umbrella: "I pick it up and open the umbrella just as it starts to rain." When the dreamer finishes telling the dream, he or she should ask a question to the others. For example, Julie asked, "What does it mean when a clown turns into an umbrella?"

Nighttime Notes

After the dream is recounted, and the dreamer asks his or her question, the guide might suggest that everyone take a few moments to consider what they've heard. Then, before trying to answer the dreamer's questions, the others should ask any questions that came to mind when they heard the dream. They should avoid making any interpretation until everyone has had a chance to consider the dream.

After Julie finished relating her dream, and after she'd asked her question of the group, she was peppered with questions. Was the clown friendly or frightening? What do clowns mean to you? What kind of memories do you have about clowns? And what do umbrellas mean to you?

Interviewing a Dreamer

Here's a list of generic questions you might ask someone who has related a dream:

- What were your feelings in the dream?
- Is there anything familiar about these feelings?
- How do you feel about the characters and events in the dream?
- What part of the dream stands out?
- Which characters struck a chord with you? Why?
- What do you associate with the main image in the dream?

In Julie's case, the answers to the questions were revealing. It turned out that she had an uncle who was a professional clown, and she could remember seeing him use an umbrella in his act. But she hadn't seen him for several years, and she still didn't know what the dream meant.

After all the questions are asked, members of the group can help interpret the dream. Remember to preface your interpretations politely, with the comment, "If it were my dream . . ." In this case, someone suggested, "If it were my dream, I'd say that the uncle was going to protect you from something, since you see umbrellas as protection."

With that comment, Julie, who was a senior, suddenly understood the dream. She hesitated, but finally told everyone that her father had nearly lost his business because of the economy, and he'd taken out loans to cover his losses. Now Julie was concerned that her parents might not be able to afford to pay her college expenses. She'd been afraid to bring up the topic because her parents were under a lot of stress and she didn't want to upset them any further.

Her uncle, however, was financially well off and didn't have any children. Then she remembered that her uncle had told her that he planned to help her pay for college. The dream, she realized, was a reminder that she had protection. She would still be able to go to college.

When everyone has told a dream, and the group has discussed the last one, you can close the session with a simple ritual. You might hold hands and give thanks for everything that the members of the group have gained in their time together. Then the leader or facilitator should blow out the candle.

Dream Experiments

Between sessions, you and your friends might try experiments in group dreaming. Just before closing the session you might suggest that everyone try incubating the same dream. For example, everyone might try to meet during a dream at a specific place. The next morning, write down what you dreamed, and don't tell anyone else in the group about it until you get together for your next dream group meeting.

Alternately, you might try to meet someone from the group in a dream. There have been instances where two people have reported sharing a dream this way, with each remembering the same conversation. In one case, in a report by Rosemary Ellen Guiley, author of *Dreamwork for the Soul,* a woman named Donna recalled meeting her friend, Anne, in a dream in which they were investigating a haunted house. Donna couldn't help asking Anne why she was wearing such a silly looking nightie. The next day, Anne recalled everything that happened in the dream. She added, "By the way, it's a new nightshirt."

Nighttime Notes

Before going to sleep, one member of the group can send a message or image to the others. That night, the group can look for the message in their dreams. Later, when the group meets again, everyone can try to identify the symbol or message that was sent.

There are also other experiments you can try with one or more partners. For example, you can work together to incubate a dream as a way of finding an answer to a difficult or annoying problem. If your group is ambitious, you can try to share a vision of a better world through your dreams. Some dream groups attempt to dream about world peace. It might be better to take a smaller step. Imagine that your group sets out to dream of a cease fire in an unstable country where violence and unrest are an everyday occurrence. A day later, a cease fire is called. The civil war is not over, but it's a step in the right direction.

Did your group have anything to do with it? Who knows? What we do know is that you and the others in your group set out to dream of a cease fire, and one came to pass.

Dream Telepathy Experiment—Identifying an Object
Here's a step-by-step procedure for a dream telepathy experiment you can try with the members of your group.

1. Pick someone from the group to be the sender. Everyone else will be receivers. Choose the day when you want to try

the experiment. You might check what happens when you try it on two successive nights.

2. The sender should pick an object, making sure to keep it secret from the receivers. Avoid any obvious choices that the others might guess. The object should be oddly shaped or unusual in some respect. That will make it easier to identify in the dream, and there won't be any confusion. A bright pink ceramic frog sitting cross-legged in a straw hat would be a better choice than a softball or a plastic glass. When you're starting out, avoid drawings or photos. Stick with the actual object.

3. On the night (or nights) of the experiment, the sender focuses on the object before going to bed. Let's say you're the sender. Hold the object, if possible, while thinking about it. Describe it in your mind. What does it mean to you? Think about any emotional links you have to the object. Where did it come from? How did it come into your possession?

4. Meanwhile, as they get ready for bed, the receivers should prepare to dream the object. If you're a receiver, you might create an affirmation, telling yourself over and over that you'll see the object clearly in a dream. Make sure you also tell yourself that you'll remember your dreams.

5. In the morning (or when they wake up), the receivers record their dream or dreams in the usual manner. If you're a receiver, examine your dream recollection. Look for an unusual object, something that stands out. Your dream may feel different in a way that makes it stand out from other dreams you remember. The images might appear brighter or sharper somehow, or maybe the colors have more punch than they normally do.

6. Start out aiming to simply describe the object. Include as much detail as you can without trying to say what it is. Describe the object's texture, its color, its shape. Once you've described it as completely as you can, then you should attempt to identify it. The reason for using this method is to keep your mind from waking up and jumping straight to a familiar conclusion about the identity of the dream object. Let's say you dreamed about a gaping dark hole with white shiny objects hanging down from the top and growing up from the bottom. If you try to make the identification right away, you might say you were in an underground cavern filled with stalagmites and stalactites. But that's not the only possibility. Maybe instead of a cave, you were looking inside the gaping mouth of a giant, long-toothed alligator!

7. Don't tell anyone in the group about your dream until the group meets. It might be a good idea for everyone to turn in their descriptions of the target to the sender. That way no one will be influenced when the sender reveals the target to the group.

In my experience working with a group in dream telepathy experiments, the descriptions can be accurate even when the exact target selected is wrong. For example, if someone sends an image of a forest, usually nobody makes that precise identification. But a few group members might talk about "something green and expansive." Someone else might describe arms with rough skin, and another person might describe long fingers reaching into the earth. On one particular target night, three out of five people dreamed of flowers. The target featured two women in traditional Japanese dress, standing by a flowering tree.

I learned an important lesson from those experiments. Your dreams are not only windows to your inner self, but they are also a means of connecting deeply with others. You might discover something similar from your own dream-sharing experiences. In dream work, we are all adventurers exploring the landscape of inner space, of a place where virtually anything can happen and often does.

Dog

Devotion, loyalty, a true friend. Also instinct, emotions. On the negative side, the metaphor could be "He follows me around like a dog." A guard dog might relate to protecting property.

Part 2

More on Dreams

Then suddenly I detach myself from the windowsill on which I am lying, and in the same reclining position fly slowly over the lane, over the houses, and then over the Golden Horn in the direction of Stamboul.

—P. D. OUSPENSKY, *A NEW MODEL OF THE UNIVERSE*

Seven

Common Dream Themes

All dreams are given for the benefit of the individual, would he but interpret them correctly.

—Edgar Cayce

Hey, have you ever dreamed about falling or flying? How about suddenly discovering you were naked in public? Or having your teeth fall out? If so, you're not alone. These are a few common dream themes that most of us experience at one time or another. They're important to consider because they relate to our day-to-day experiences. They are connected to what happens to us at school, at home, with our friends. Sometimes they express fears or anxieties. Other times, they relate to our joys and triumphs.

These themes are *common* because a lot of people experience them in their dreams. But they may also be common if you have the same dream, with slight variations in plot, over and over again. Dream researcher Gayle Delaney says that common dreams represent a recurring theme or problem in our lives. "Oftentimes this theme is one we share with many other people. By understanding our particular version of a common dream, we can resolve a recurring problem and at the same time appreciate the fact that many of us at one time or another share similar difficulties in living."

Okay, let's take a close look at several common dream themes. That way you can get a better understanding of what they mean. Let's start out by deciding which common dream themes, if any, you can recall dreaming yourself.

Your Common Dream Themes

Take a look at this list of common dream themes. Which ones are familiar? Check the appropriate box.

Common Dream Themes	Never/not sure	Once	Repeatedly or many times
Flying dreams			
Falling dreams			
Taking a plane, train, or bus			
Losing keys, wallet, purse, luggage			
Being at school and/or taking a test			
Discovering you are naked			
Feeling teeth falling out			
Finding money			
Hunting for/finding a bathroom			
Swimming, floating, being in or around water			
Dying, witnessing death of another person			

Flying Dreams

Flying can be one of the greatest things you can experience in a dream. It's so exhilarating to feel like you're just soaring away, so light and completely under control. It's a sensation you should savor and remember. You can fly around your room, around the neighborhood, or even to the stars.

Sigmund Freud thought that flying dreams had something to do with a person's driving desire to have a close relationship. But today, most therapists favor Carl Jung's explanation that such dreams are related to a sense of breaking free of restrictions. It's easy to make dream-related puns that support Jung's theory. After all, flying is such an "uplifting" experience. In fact, you could say that when you fly, you're "rising" above your problems.

Nighttime Notes

Some dream researchers say that flying dreams indicate a vivid imagination and a sense of courage. For example, if you made up imaginary worlds when you were younger, you might also have experienced flying dreams that reflected your sense of confidence and personal freedom.

Flying dreams may continue into your teens and even adulthood. However, for many people, these dreams stop at some point around the teen years. That might reflect increasing concerns about what others think about you. It's natural for us to want to fit in with the crowd to some extent. But remember, following the group all of the time tends to suck your creative juices dry. A desire to fit in may be keeping you grounded instead of helping you to soar—both in your dreaming life and your waking life. You may also experience a more grounded feeling as you get older and take on more responsibilities—homework, school activities, maybe even an after-school job. You're probably also becoming more and more annoyed by the rules and restrictions set up by your parents and maybe even testing their tolerance. In this respect, getting grounded takes on new meaning!

As you near high school graduation and prepare for the new and exciting things in your future, your dreams of flying might begin again. Take the example of Ben, a seventeen-year-old senior, who dreamed of flying after receiving a letter of acceptance to Duke University.

Controlled Flight

I was running and with each step my strides were getting longer and longer. Then I was lifting up off the ground and remaining in the air and I could control my movements. It felt great and I wondered why I'd forgotten that I could fly. I remember flying when I was younger. When I woke up, I almost leaped out of bed. I felt like I could do anything I wanted.

Ben said that he'd also dreamed of flying after he'd gotten his SAT scores, but he'd forgotten about it until his latest flying dream. He thought he must have had other flying dreams when he was younger, too.

The Dream Interview

The best way to find out what your flying dream means is to interview yourself. Imagine that you're a reporter. Ask yourself these questions:

- How did you feel while you were flying?
- Are you running away from something or someone, or are you just having a good time?
- Do you have any trouble taking off or holding your altitude?
- Does this dream feel familiar, like you've done it before?

- Do you feel in control of your flight?
- Can you relate the feeling of flying to anything that is happening in your waking life?

The meaning of your dream has a lot to do with how you feel while you're flying. Whether it's an exhilarating or frightening experience, try to connect the sensation to something going on in your waking life. If someone is chasing you in a flying dream and you're out of control in your flight, the flight itself could be a pun, as in "taking flight." Such a situation could be about a bad relationship. Someone is "pursuing you"—another pun—and you can't seem to stop this person's advances. The whole situation is out of control.

Nighttime Notes

But usually a flying dream is joyful, a thrilling episode in your dream life to be treasured for the experience itself, and it usually relates to positive changes in your waking life.

Falling Dreams

Falling is just about the most common dream theme. Though falling dreams can be scary, no one ever dies in a falling dream. You can hit the ground and live to tell about it. Falling dreams can come in many different forms—sometimes you're pushed, other times you trip. You might fall from a building, off a mountain, or out of an airplane. A falling dream may contain an important message telling you to watch your step. Or it might suggest that you're moving in the wrong direction, possibly on a dangerous path. Such a dream also could be a metaphor for a fall from grace or falling on hard times, like coming home with bad grades and getting grounded. It could even relate to something really innocuous, like the fall season.

Fifteen-year-old Aaron was worried about his report card when he dreamed of tumbling off a roof.

Falling from a Building

I'm on the roof of a building with a bunch of my friends. It's like a party and there's Spanish music playing, but I'm not having fun. I'm feeling sort of worried. I look over the edge of the building. Suddenly, a gust of wind catches me by surprise and blows me over the side. I tumble over and over. The ground is jumping up toward me when I wake up. I'm sweating and gasping for breath. I'm so glad it was a dream.

Aaron was worried he was going to get a D in Spanish. He knew that he would lose a lot of his privileges. He would be staying home on weekends for the next semester. Of course, the dream reflected his feelings rather than the true nature of his situation. He ended up with a C, which didn't please his parents, either. But he promised to study harder, and they didn't punish him.

The Dream Interview

Here are some questions to consider about your dream of falling:

- Do you know why you're falling?
- How do you feel about the fall?
- What caused you to fall in the dream?
- What event or events led up to your fall?
- Is there anything in your life that reminds you of the fall and the incidents leading up to it?

Falling dreams usually relate to our worries and concerns. They're not dangerous, but they can be frightening. Just remember that the message behind a falling dream might be a warning that you should heed.

Taking a Plane, Train, or Bus

The important thing about dreams about mass transportation—trains, planes, and buses—is what you are doing in the dream. Are you waiting in the station? Are you worried about missing a plane? Are you feeling lost and confused by all the train lines in the station? Are you traveling really fast, feeling the thrill of the speed?

You might have such a dream at the end of summer vacation as school is about to begin again. That's often a time of uncertainty, especially if you're going to a new school. You might misplace your ticket or worry about catching the plane or train or bus on time.

Nighttime Notes

Dreams of travel can often reflect the difficult changes that come with growing up. If you're dealing with uncertainty in your life, you might find that you have more travel dreams.

As a metaphor, taking trains might indicate that you're "in training." Likewise, waiting in a train or a bus station might relate to concerns about not moving ahead, in other words, being "stationary." Travel dreams might also represent the journey of your life.

Eighteen-year-old Tracy dreamed of finding herself in a busy bus station after an argument with her father about her plans for college.

The Bus Station

I went to bed last night feeling angry at my father after we talked about college and I know it had something to do with my dream. He spent almost an hour trying to convince me to study for a law degree so I can be a lawyer, just like him and my older brother. But art is my real love and I think being a lawyer would be borrrrrr-ing. Finally, he said, "We'll talk about this later."

So I dreamed that I was sitting in a bus station with lots of people walking back and forth. It was very confusing, especially since I didn't know what bus I was supposed to take or even where I was going. I just sat there feeling lost and confused. Then I heard someone say, "Which direction art thou going?" That's when I woke up.

The dream is clearly a reflection of Tracy's conversation with her father. She's feeling confused about her future. The bus station is symbolic of a crossroads for her. The use of the archaic phrase "art thou" suggests that her interest in art is at the heart of her concern.

The Dream Interview

Here are some questions to consider about your dream of traveling:

- What's the most important thing you're doing in your travel dream?
- How do you feel about it?
- Are you traveling with anyone?
- Do you know where you're going?
- If you're having difficulties on your journey, do you know why?
- Does the dream remind you of something going on in your waking life?

A travel dream involving public transportation usually deals with some aspect of how you are moving ahead in your life. The way you act and feel, as well as other elements of the dream itself, help determine its meaning. For instance, transportation dreams are sometimes combined with the next common dream theme, that is, losing something of value.

Losing Keys, Wallet, Purse, Luggage

What do these items mean to you? Usually, they relate to security and identity. These disturbing incidents sometimes take place within a travel dream.

Such dreams might occur during or after a divorce or move, changing school, or beginning a new experience.

Nighttime Notes

Losing keys, a billfold, a purse, luggage, or other valuables might indicate a worry about your security, your sense of identity or belonging, and your self-worth.

Thirteen-year-old Sean had recurring dreams for months about losing his parents and misplacing his plane ticket.

Lost in Airport

I'm wandering around the airport. My mom went one way and my dad the other and I don't know where they are. The plane's about to leave and I still can't find them. A man in a uniform wants my ticket, but I think I lost it. He asks if I'm traveling with my mother or father. Then I wake up.

In Sean's case, the meaning was clear. His parents were in the process of getting a divorce, and he felt like he'd lost everything. When things settled down and he began visiting his father on weekends, the dreams stopped.

The Dream Interview

To find out what your dream about losing something of value means, ask yourself these questions:

- What does the lost object mean to you? What is its purpose?
- Is it related to your identity, to something you possess?
- How did you feel in the dream about losing the object?
- Is there anything going on in your life that makes you feel the same way?

Dreams of losing something important make you feel uncomfortable. It's the way your inner self gets you to look at your fear or concern about losing your sense of who you are, what's important to you, and possibly where you are going.

Taking a Test

No doubt you are used to taking tests. As a student, you take them all the time. You might be surprised to find out that it's common for adults to dream of taking tests. These dreams usually start in the teen years. Usually, in the dream, you're totally unprepared for the test. It might be a classroom test, or you might realize you have to give a speech or go on stage to perform. Whatever it is, you're not ready. You haven't studied or done your homework. You're afraid of failing.

Sound familiar? Unlike some of the other dream themes we've discussed, the dream of taking a test can have a very literal interpretation. You actually may be concerned about being unprepared for a test, a speech, or a performance. When you're out of school, it could relate to some of life's other tests. Many adults call this dream the "college dream." They suddenly find themselves back in college and unprepared for a big test—they might even realize with a horrible sinking feeling that they haven't even been going to class. Such a dream might occur if the person is concerned about being qualified for some new challenge in his or her life. This might be a new job or a promotion.

After eighth grade, Zoe stopped playing the cello. Her family moved to a small town, where the high school had a band but no orchestra. She didn't want to start her music lessons over with a wind instrument. During ninth grade, she started having the following dream.

Stage Fright

I'm walking on stage with my cello. The lights are bright and I'm sweating already. I know the auditorium is full and everyone is waiting for me to play. There's a chair for me in the center of the stage, but I notice there's no written music, just an empty stand. I stop in my tracks. I don't know what I'm going to play. I don't have any music with me. I'm totally unprepared. I panic and run off stage. I wake up with my heart pounding.

Zoe said that she's had the dream several times, usually a couple of days before a big test or an oral presentation. That's when she knows that she needs to get prepared.

The Dream Interview

If you've had a dream about a test that you were unprepared to take, ask yourself these questions:

- Look at your schedule. Is there a test coming up that you've forgotten about?
- If not, what significant event is taking place in your life?
- Are you being tested related to the event?
- How prepared are you to deal with it?
- What lessons can you learn from the dream?
- How can you be better prepared?

Discovering You Are Naked

While dreams about being unprepared for a test might have a literal meaning, you don't have to worry about that if you dream of being naked in public. These dreams are definitely symbolic. Maybe you've discovered the "naked truth" about something. If you're comfortable and not embarrassed by your nudity, the dream might mean that you're shedding an old role, represented by your old clothes, and becoming someone new.

Depending on how you feel about being naked, it might relate to anxiety about something in your life that's being exposed. Or it might relate to a wish for more exposure of something in your life. The following dream is one such example.

Nick, a high school senior, was confused by his recurring dream of being nude in public.

Naked with Art

In the dreams, I'm usually walking around naked in a crowd of people. In every dream up to now, I feel embarrassed. I'm trying to hide or find some clothes. But no one seems to pay any attention to me.

In this dream, though, I'm not at all concerned about my nudity. I just don't care. I'm also carrying a painting that's wrapped up in brown paper and I'm thinking about how the painting is covered and I'm not when my art teacher comes up to me. She points to the picture and says, "Aren't you forgetting something?" That's when I wake up.

After this dream, Nick realized that the dreams had something to do with his interest in attending an art college after he graduated. In order to be accepted in the program, he had to appear before a review committee and talk about himself and show samples of his art. In other words, he would be exposing himself.

When asked what his art teacher meant by her comment, he suddenly knew the answer. "I've been worried about showing my best work to the committee, because I thought it might be too radical for their tastes. It's really an expression of myself and how I see the world. Now I realize I can't hide myself anymore. Besides, I'm proud of my work. My teacher is telling me I have to uncover my art."

The Dream Interview

If you've dreamed of being nude in public, ask yourself these questions:

- What were you doing while you were nude?
- If other people are in the dream, how do they relate to your nudity?

- How did you feel about not wearing clothes?
- Are you keeping something under wraps that needs to be exposed?
- Can you relate the way you feel to anything in your life?

Teeth Falling Out

Nighttime Notes
When teeth fall out in a dream, which is surprisingly common, it reflects a concern about weakness.

If you've lost your teeth in a dream, it may mean you need to visit the dentist, but it could also signify something completely different. As symbols, teeth are related to strength, power, or aggressiveness, as in "sinking your teeth" into something. Such dreams can also relate to an inability to communicate or to grasp a situation. Usually these dreams leave you feeling disturbed, but they don't create the fears and anxiety of a nightmare.

Dream researcher Ann Faraday notes that her own loss-of-teeth dreams almost always reflect her feelings that she has "lost face" or "spoiled her self-image" in some way during the day, usually giving in to her fears. Losing face can also relate to finding yourself in an embarrassing situation or a potentially embarrassing one.

Eighteen-year-old Sara reported this dream about teeth.

Losing My Teeth

I'm out on a date with a guy and I like him. We're sitting in his car and he wants to kiss me. But before he does, I run inside to brush my teeth. There's no toothbrush in this bathroom so I wipe my teeth with my fingers. As I touch one of my teeth, it falls out. Each tooth I touch falls out. I go back to the car feeling panicked, but the guy doesn't seem to notice that anything's different.

91

Sara related the dream to a situation in her life. She's been dating someone she's known as a friend for several years. He wants to get serious with her, but she still thinks of him as a friend. She wants to end the relationship, but she doesn't want to hurt his feelings.

The Dream Interview

If you've lost your teeth in a dream, ask yourself these questions:

- What's going on in the dream when you lose your teeth?
- Is someone else in the dream? If so, do you know the person? How does he or she relate to you losing your teeth?
- How did you feel about losing your teeth—panicked, upset, worried, resigned?
- Is there something in your life that's causing you to feel a loss of power or a sense of "losing face"?

Finding Money

If you dream of finding money, you can always hope it's a precognitive dream and you're about to discover a hidden cache. But chances are the dream was symbolic. Actually, a lot of people dream of finding money. As a teen, I used to dream of digging under the trunk of a large oak tree and finding piles of old coins. Such dreams usually suggest that you're searching for something of value or uncovering it.

Nighttime Notes

Discovering gold coins might indicate success in a matter at hand. Ancient coins could relate to something from your past that is coming to a head, probably in your favor.

Here's a dream recorded by Tara, a fifteen-year-old, who has high hopes of getting a horse. If you've been reading closely, you've probably noticed by now that horses figure into a number of dreams reported on these pages. That's because many of the teens whose dreams are included here live in an equestrian community in Florida.

Treasure Hunt

I'm digging into the ground underneath a shed. I'm finding coins that look old and tarnished, like gold doubloons. But I notice that they have horse heads on one side. I keep digging and find more and more. I stuff them into a big cloth bag. Other people are looking, too, but they don't seem to see the coins. It's like a treasure hunt and I keep finding the coins. I feel great about it.

Note that others don't see the coins, which indicates that what Tara holds as valuable isn't necessarily shared by others. When that was suggested to her, Tara laughed and immediately agreed. Some of her friends don't share her love for horseback riding or her wish to own a horse of her own. "The horse head on the coin made me think that everything will work out as I've hoped."

When she was asked about what she thought the shed meant, she realized it wasn't a shed. "It's a stable with stalls for horses."

The Dream Interview

If you've had a dream in which you've discovered money, ask yourself these questions:

- How did you feel when you made the discovery?
- What discoveries are you making or hope to make in your waking life?

- Do others value what you do?
- If you're finding coins, what do they look like?
- What do you do with the coins?

Water Dreams

Dreams about water are as common as water itself! However, the significance of a water dream will vary, depending on the circumstances of the individual dream. Stormy waters can relate to strong emotions. Floating comfortably in a pool comes with a pleasant, weightless sensation. It might suggest that you need to take a break from things that are burdening you.

Flowing water might indicate undercurrents in your life, or it could point to deep meanings related to the unconscious mind. If you're drowning in a dream, you need to look for possible metaphors. What conditions in your life leave you feeling as if you're "over your head," "out of your depth," or simply as though you're drowning? If you're diving into water, are you immersing yourself in something in your life? How do you feel about it in the dream?

Barbara, a sixteen-year-old, recalled a series of water dreams she had when she was fourteen.

I'm Drowning
I dreamed that I was drowning over and over again. Sometimes I would be in a bathtub, other times it was a lake. The last time was the most dramatic, because I drowned in the ocean. The undertow just swept me out to sea. After each dream I would wake up and gasp for air, glad that I was alive. Shortly after the last dream, we moved and I haven't had a drowning dream in two years.

During the time that Barbara was dreaming of drowning, her family was undergoing difficult times. Her father had lost his job, and her mother's income wasn't enough to support the family. As a result, Barbara felt the pinch. She was transferred from an expensive private school to a public school. Instead of getting whatever she wanted, she learned not even to ask for things because the answer would probably be no. Her family was drowning in debt, and her parents talked about filing for bankruptcy. It went on for months, until her father found a new job and the family moved. The move was turbulent and costly. That was when she had her last drowning dream. After that, things improved.

The Dream Interview

If you've had a dream involving water, ask yourself these questions:

- How did you relate to the water? Were you floating, drowning, observing, going with the flow, swimming, or surfing?
- How did you feel about the water? Was it comforting, overwhelming, cold, powerful, calm, flowing, clear, or murky?
- Can you relate your feelings about the water to anything taking place in your life?
- Are there other people in the dream? Is so, ask them what they're doing there. What is their purpose?

Finding a Bathroom

Another common dream theme, this one might simply mean that you need to get up and go to the bathroom. Young children who wet beds often dream that they are in the bathroom, and they are surprised when they wake up in a wet bed instead. Sometimes bathroom dreams can shock you out of your ordinary expectations, like a dream of walking into a public bathroom to find both boys and girls in there. Such dreams might suggest a desire to break out of a mold or break a taboo.

Nighttime Notes

If you're taking a shower in your dream, this might be a symbol of a need to clean up a matter in your life.

Dream researcher Cynthia Richmond recalled a series of bathroom dreams she had as a teenager. She had been very active in her church, but gradually she became disenchanted as she was discouraged from exploring deeper spiritual questions. She was expected to memorize the standard answers and not question them. She began having dreams of a minister squatting over an old-fashioned chamber pot. She realized that her dreaming self was telling her that the perspective she was receiving was outdated. That led her to a wider exploration of religion and spiritual values.

The Dream Interview

If you've determined your dream isn't simply the call of nature, ask yourself these questions:

- What's going on in your bathroom dream? Are you relieving yourself or maybe taking a shower?
- If it's a public bathroom, who else is present?
- Is there something you need to eliminate or cleanse from your life? What's blocking you from doing so?
- If someone else is in the bathroom, what does that person mean to you?
- How did you feel when you woke up: anxious, relieved, cleansed?

Death Dreams

If you've dreamed of dying, you can relax. In all likelihood, it doesn't mean that you're going to die—at least not any time soon. In fact, most people who are about to die dream about their life, not their death. Dreaming of your death actually might mean that you are undergoing a transformation of some sort. For a teen, it might be moving to another town or city and changing schools. Or, for older teens, it might relate to the transformation to adulthood, possibly triggered by graduating and leaving home for college.

Nighttime Notes

Many dreams about death involve car crashes. In these cases, the car serves a metaphor for where you're going in life and how the journey is unfolding.

For seventeen-year-old Jim, a roller coaster figured prominently in his death dream. It underscored the need to end a relationship with a fifteen-year-old girl.

Roller Coaster

Heather and I are at the county fair. She's excited like a kid, eating cotton candy and running from ride to ride, dragging me along. I don't like crowds and all the noise and wish we could leave.

She wants to go on the roller coaster, but I don't. We argue about it and I'm embarrassed. Just to keep her quiet, I go on the ride with her. I hate the roller coaster with everyone screaming and the idiots holding their arms up in the air. Heather clutches my arm and shrieks like a five-year-old. As our car speeds down one of the steep slopes, Heather's seat restraint suddenly snaps and she's hurled out of the car. I see her shooting like a missile through the air and know it's going to kill her. I feel relieved.

When I woke up, I was shocked at my lack of emotion and couldn't go back to sleep. But the longer I lay there, the clearer it became that Heather and I no longer enjoyed the same things. She was too immature. It just wasn't working out.

In Jim's dream, death symbolized the reality of his relationship with Heather. It was over, and Jim knew it. Even though the dream was symbolic, it was still shocking. For such dreams, there is only one relevant question to ask yourself: What kind of transformation is taking place in your life?

Stase Michaels, author of *The Bedside Guide to Dreams,* recalls a series of dreams she experienced in her late teens in which she was taking driving lessons. In each of the dreams, she barely avoided crashing. Looking back, she realized that the dreams symbolized her transformation from a shy and insecure girl to an independent and confident young woman.

Very rarely, death dreams are actually warnings. You might identify such dreams by their realistic details. If you dream of the brakes failing on your parents' car, it could be a warning rather than a symbol of feeling out of control. If the car looks exactly like your parents' car and other details are realistic, such as the highway and surroundings, it's probably a good idea to take the dream seriously. Tell your parents about your dream and suggest that the brakes get checked.

The Dream Interview

While the vast majority of death dreams are symbolic, here are some questions you might ask if you have a dream about death and are concerned that it might be a warning:

- How realistic was the dream?
- Can you describe the details of the setting?
- Did you recognize other people in the dream? Did they look like they do in your waking life?
- Is there anything going on in your life that feels like the death dream scenario?
- If you're truly concerned that it might be a warning, is there anything you can do to prevent the dream scenario from becoming a reality?

My Dream Themes

Using your dream journal, jot down a dream that belongs to one of the common dream themes. See how this theme relates to events in your own life. Think about the many different meanings a theme can have and decide what your dream means to you. Remember, don't hold back. As you interpret it, allow the dream to speak to you. Take the following steps to examine your dream:

- Decide which common theme the dream belongs to.
- Record the dream in as much detail as possible.
- Define your feelings about the dream.
- Think about the events that preceded the dream and how the dream relates to them.
- Decide on your interpretation of the dream.
- Ask yourself how your interpretation fits within the common meanings of the dream's theme. Do those meanings help you interpret your dream? Or do you find that your dream has a new and different significance?

Tiger

Aggressive and cunning behavior, power. Are you the tiger stalking its prey? Or is the tiger stalking you? If so, is there something in your life that you want to get rid of, perhaps an overinflated ego or a pattern of negativity?

Eight

Relationship Dreams

. . . I could be bounded in a nutshell and
count myself a king of infinite space, were
it not that I have bad dreams.
—WILLIAM SHAKESPEARE, *HAMLET*

et's face it. Dreams are ego trips. You are almost always the star, the main character who stays at center stage. But your dreams also feature family members, friends, classmates, and even celebrities. Sometimes these people play supporting roles, or they may be against you in some way. These dream characters are often messengers from your own unconscious mind.

When it seems as though a dream focuses on someone other than yourself, be sure to take a close look. Do you know that person or people? What do they look like? What clothes are they wearing? If you know them, do they look or act any differently from your waking image of them? How do they react toward you? Are they present in the dream as a friend, or an enemy? How do you feel about the dream characters?

An antagonist in a dream might be someone you already consider an enemy. But it might also be a good friend, someone close to you. If you and your friend aren't getting along, your dreams might reflect your state of mind regarding the person. However, if you are on friendly terms, your dreaming self might be nudging you to take a closer look at your relationship.

Nighttime Notes

Your relationship to a certain character (or characters) is the key to helping you understand the meaning of some dreams.

In the case of sixteen-year-old Jennifer, her "boyfriend" appeared in her dream, then vanished right in front of her. But that wasn't the only unusual thing about the dream.

Vanishing Boyfriend

I was waiting on a corner under a streetlight for my boyfriend to arrive. I felt excited, and the way the light was shining on me made me feel like I was standing at center stage. I heard him call my name, then I saw him coming toward me. But it was hard to see his face because of the light shining on me. Just as he got close enough to see him clearly, he faded and vanished.

He was there one moment, then gone. I looked all around for him, but couldn't find him. What really bothered me was that I never saw his face, because of the light. I started to call his name, but I couldn't think what it was. Then suddenly the dream shifted locations and I was back in my room and I could hear a telephone making a busy sound. I knew then that the boyfriend wasn't anyone, because I don't have a boyfriend. That's when I woke up.

Jennifer wished she had a boyfriend, but she recognized that the busy signal at the end of the dream was about having too much going on in her life for a boyfriend. She's a very attractive girl, who is quick-witted and involved in a lot of after-school activities. It would seem that she would have lots of opportunities for boyfriends. But the dream suggested that she was somehow blinded by the light that illuminated her.

At first, she didn't understand what that meant. But after discussing the dream, she admitted that she had a reputation of being kind of self-centered. The bright streetlight, or spotlight, might represent her ego. The dream, it seemed, was telling her that she needed to pay more attention to the interests and concerns of others. Boys probably see her as unapproachable or too impressed with herself, too self-involved. The vanishing boyfriend was a message from a deeper part of her that she needed to focus more on the interests of others.

Who Is That Person?

Using your dream journal, follow these steps to find out more about your dream characters:

- Describe the dream character in detail.
- Does the dream character remind you of someone you know well? If you can identify the person, decide how your dream version compares to your impression of the person in waking life.
- How do you feel about the character?
- Could the character represent some part of your personality that you need to look at more closely?

Meeting Celebrities

Encountering a celebrity, whether it's a movie star, famous musician, or the president of the United States, is usually a thrilling experience. It's the same way in our dreams, except you often get closer to the celebrity than you would in waking life. You might not only talk to the celebrity, but the two of you might get to hang out as if you were old friends.

If the celebrity acts as a close friend or an advisor, someone whose opinion you can trust, then the dream may be a way of giving you an important message with the celebrity as the courier. Because of his or her status, you will be ready to listen to the message, which might actually be coming from a deeper part of yourself.

Nighttime Notes

The meaning of celebrity dreams depends on what the person means to you—and, of course, on what happens in the dream. But celebrities are usually archetypal figures, modern-day heroes and heroines.

Here's a dream recorded by thirteen-year-old Christine that combines a frightening chase scene with a celebrity encounter with members of Destiny's Child.

Running Away

I was shopping with my sister, going from store to store. We were very happy. Then, out of the corner of my eye, I saw several people dressed in black running toward us. There were four of them, three men and a woman. I immediately knew they were after us. I ran into a store with my sister and we hid behind a rack of purses.

I didn't even realize at first that Beyonce, Kelly, and Michelle from Destiny's Child were in the store shopping for purses. As my sister called our mom on her cell phone, the people dressed in black charged into the store. To my relief, Beyonce, Kelly, and Michelle saved us when they told them that we went the other way.

So we thanked them for their help and left the store using the back door, which led outside. At that exact moment, I saw my mom's car in the distance. She was speeding toward us. My sister and I quickly climbed into the car. As we left, we saw the people in black coming out the same door. They knew we'd left the mall and they were very upset.

The next morning, my alarm clock woke me at 7:15 A.M. I was well rested, but I had mixed feelings about the dream. I was disturbed by the people in black and asked myself why we were running from them. But I also felt happy that I spent time with my sister and saw Destiny's Child. I also felt that I was being adventurous by being pursued by danger.

The last comment of Christine's might be the key to the dream. The trip to the mall was an adventure. They were chased by dangerous people and encountered celebrities, who—like heroines—saved them from danger. If there is a message from Destiny's Child, it's that Christine has the ability to detect danger and escape from it before it's too late. She, too, can play the role of heroine.

Celebrity Quiz

Here are some questions you can ask yourself about your close encounter with a celebrity:

- What happens in your dream related to the celebrity?
- Does the celebrity recognize you or brush you off?
- What does the person mean to you? What is he or she like?
- Does the person remind you of anyone in your life?
- Does the person have a message for you?

The way you feel about the celebrity and the way the celebrity acts are two key elements to understanding such a dream. If the celebrity reminds you of someone in your life, it may be that the dream is more about your relationship with that person than the celebrity. Finally, pay close attention to any message the celebrity relays to you.

Dreams of Family

Probably your most frequent dream visitors are members of your family. If you've been recording your dreams, look back over the last ten and see how often a family member has made an appearance.

When a family member does show up in a dream, take note of the role the person plays.

- Is he or she helpful or troublesome?
- Does the same person appear over and over again?
- Do you react to this person with love, anger, indifference?
- How do you feel about the person in waking life?

Sometimes dreams can be a way of expressing love for family members that you don't often show in daily life. But other times shocking things happen. You might get so angry that you assault your mother or your brother in a dream. Alternately, a family member might blow up at you, attack you, or even kill you. These violent dream episodes are your way of dealing with unexpressed feelings. Nobody wants dramatic family scenes like that in waking life, but in a dream, these experiences can help bring difficult matters to the surface. Whatever the issue, it may be time to openly express your feelings. If that's not possible, it might be a good idea to talk to a school counselor or another trusted adult.

Dreams featuring parents might express feelings related to recent discussions or events, such as a divorce or remarriage, if things like that have arisen in your life. Consider the following dream recorded by twelve-year-old Anne (not her real name).

Nighttime Notes

When your mother or father appears in a dream, they usually relate to some aspect of your actual relationship with the parent.

The Crocodile

It was about dusk when my dad, his girlfriend, Carla, and I were outside his house by the canal. Everything had a dark tint to it, including the trees and the canal. We were talking when Carla saw a baby crocodile. All of a sudden, she burst out, "Oh, how cute. I want to feed it."

My dad and I thought this was rather funny, so I said, "I wouldn't do that if I were you." But she didn't listen and instead threw a piece of bread at it. All of a sudden, several huge crocodiles lunged at her and bit off her finger. That's when I woke up laughing.

That dream suggests that Anne isn't entirely happy with her father's girlfriend, a common feeling for children and teens who have to deal with a substitute parent. Anne warns Carla about the danger of getting too close, which could mean that in her waking life, she's skeptical about developing a relationship with Carla. Anne doesn't know her very well and still feels an allegiance to her mother. So she warns Carla to keep her distance. When Carla ignores the warning, she loses a finger. In laughing at the outcome, Anne seems to be satisfied with her warning and not particularly concerned about Carla, who will never replace her mother. As you can see, the action in the dream is a metaphor for the parental situation in Anne's life.

Dreams of Friends

Dreams of friends and schoolmates are often more complicated than dreams featuring family members because such dream characters are often symbolic.

Nighttime Notes

When you dream of a friend, try to think of what that friend means to you.

How is the person acting in the dream? If the dream character is not someone you know well, then consider if the person's looks or behavior remind you of anything about yourself. You should also consider whether the character reminds you of someone else who is close to you.

If the person is supportive, he or she might represent a valuable part of your personality that you might not recognize. On the other hand, if the person antagonizes you, he or she might represent someone close to you who acts in the same manner. Or maybe that's a part of you, too!

If that's the case, the friend represents a message from your unconscious mind telling you something about your personality that you need to change. Here's one such example from a dream recorded by fifteen-year-old Mike.

Fatty 1, 2, and 3

I was on my skateboard practicing my moves when Jimmy, a friend of mine, came over with his board. We were just messing around, like we usually do, when the three kids who live next door came outside to watch us. Jimmy stopped right in front of them, turned to me, and grinned. "Hey, here's Fatty 1, Fatty 2, and Fatty 3, all together. Hi, Plumpos!" Then he laughed and skated away. Their faces fell. A moment ago, they'd looked happy and curious. Now they seemed sad and hurt. That made me so mad that I shoved Jimmy as he came up to me and he fell off his skateboard.

"You didn't have to say that!"

He looked up at me in surprise. "Say what?"

That made me even madder, and I was about to kick him when suddenly I woke up. I was sweating and feeling really angry because those kids hadn't done anything to him.

After describing the dream, Mike realized that his friend wasn't really much like the Jimmy he knew in waking life. In fact, he couldn't remember Jimmy ever making fun of other kids. As he looked more closely at the dream, Mike was surprised to realize that his anger was about his own behavior. In fact, he admitted that on more than one occasion, he had made fun of the neighbor kids about their weight.

Dreams of Strangers

Strangers who appear in your dreams sometimes act like they know you well, and you might act the same way toward them. In fact, you might not realize that you don't know the person until you wake up. So what does that mean? Maybe you have dream friends that you don't know in your waking life! That could be, but these strangers can also represent people you *do* know. They can also symbolize aspects of your own personality.

Nighttime Notes

Strangers in dreams can be friendly or menacing. Even though you don't know the person, it's usually easy to tell whether the dream character is on your side or working against you.

Some strangers might be advisors who have wisdom or important information to share. Others may be ready to slit your throat or pummel you in a dark alley. Whatever their role, they usually serve a purpose, or they wouldn't be in your dreams.

In the following dream, thirteen-year-old Nicole is pursued by a masked stranger.

Fighting for Survival

My parents were going to Home Depot. My brother was annoying me so I went with them. I tagged along, following my parents down one aisle after another. As we were walking up toward the cash register, a man in black clothes who was wearing a mask pulled me aside and covered my mouth. He pointed a gun at my head and mumbled something about money. My body went stiff and I thought I was going to die. Then, remembering the Tae Kwon Do that I'd learned, I elbowed him in the stomach and knocked the gun out of his hand.

Then I ran and told my parents what happened. At first, they didn't believe me until they heard a shot fired. We dropped to the floor and crawled for the door. We ran outside to our car and sped away, but the man saw us and followed in a rusty old car. We lost him and went home, but he somehow found us and shot the door down. We ran out the back door, but he heard the door slam and followed us. We dashed over to our neighbor's house and called the police. But the man came right in the house and began searching for us. When he went upstairs, we ran out the front door.

We jumped in our car and headed over to a friend's house. Again, the man followed us and we called the police again. We tried to lose him in the neighborhood and hid our car in our friend's garage. But the masked stranger still found us. He knocked down the door and looked everywhere for us. We were hiding behind the couch, the only place he didn't check. Seconds later, the cops barged in and arrested the man upstairs. After that day, we were afraid to go back to Home Depot.

In Nicole's dream, the reference to Home Depot held a clue. While it seemed that the masked man was a stranger, he might've represented a side of Nicole's personality that she wanted to keep hidden. Carl Jung called that part of our personality the "shadow" side. He believed that it was important to confront the shadow and bring it into the light, even if we didn't like what we saw. Using this interpretation, the masked man may have been delivering a message from Nicole's unconscious mind telling her she needed to look closer at her shadow side and make some changes.

Interviewing the Stranger

If you're having difficulty understanding the role of the stranger, you can use the dream interview technique—the one we talked about in Chapter 4—to better understand the stranger's place in your dream. Here are some questions you can ask the character you're concerned about. Even if you know the person in waking life, act as if he or she is unfamiliar to you. Imagine the character is sitting in a chair across from you as you conduct the interview.

- Who are you? Describe yourself in a few words.
- What are you doing in my dream?
- Do you represent someone I know?
- Do you represent a part of me? If so, what is it?
- What can I learn from your appearance?

Feather

Flight, connection with the heavens, the divine. In Native American cultures, feathers were sacred and related to healing and other rituals. In particular, an eagle feather represents strength, pride, protection, and transformation. A peacock feather represents beauty and insight.

Nine

Nightmares

All that we see or seem is but a dream within a dream.

—EDGAR ALLAN POE,
A DREAM WITHIN A DREAM

Have you ever woken up from a terrible nightmare in the middle of the night, sweating and gasping for breath? Even though you know the nightmare is over, that eerie feeling may hang on for a while, probably until you fall asleep again or maybe even until you start your next day. As a result, nightmares can also leave you feeling angry, guilty, sad, or even depressed. The fear and anxiety they cause puts nightmares in a different category from other dreams.

While everyone has nightmares once in a while, some people have them more than others. Some people even have recurring nightmares. The themes vary widely, but many times people find themselves being chased. Teens and adults are commonly pursued by an unknown male figure, while children are often chased by an animal or monster.

While nightmares and regular dreams may have similar scenarios, nightmares are distinguished by the intense feeling of fear and dread they cause. A lot of times they also create a spine-chilling, haunted sensation. You usually wake up feeling relieved that it was just a dream.

The following is a nightmare recorded by twelve-year-old Harrison that involved lizards, or "curly tails."

The Curly Tail Barbecue

It all started with my mom tucking me into bed. We were talking about the curly tails that hang around our patio. See the reason we have so many is that my mom feeds them chicken or steak, whatever she is cooking that night on the barbecue, and they fight over the pieces. My sister came into the room and said that if we keep feeding them, they are going to get bigger and bigger. We all laughed and then my mom said goodnight and I fell asleep. That's when the curly tail barbecue began.

There I was on my patio with my family and a good friend, but we were as small as the curly tails and they were having the barbecue. They had chef's hats on and they were sitting in chairs talking and laughing. Then I realized they were laughing at us, chasing us, and trying to catch us. Everything was turned around. Just then a baby curly tail caught me and held me tightly in its claws.

I was afraid it was going to eat me or put me on the barbecue. His eyes were big and glassy and his teeth looked sharp. But he was smiling and he tagged me and said, "You're it." He wanted me to chase him. Even though he was about forty times bigger than me, I went along with it. I started running after him and everything seemed so big and scary. The blades of grass were taller than me and I was quickly exhausted. I stopped to rest and felt something cold scoop me up. I realized it was a spatula and suddenly I thought I was going to be the dinner.

There I was sitting on this cold spatula and wondering what would happen next. Well, to my surprise, another curly tail picked up a spatula and they started flipping me back and forth. It was hard on my bones and I was afraid they were going to drop me. Then it happened. I felt myself falling toward the ground and that was when I woke up. I felt disoriented, but I was relieved that it was just a dream and I was the right size.

Nightmares often are related to your psychological fears. For example, if you're afraid of speaking in front of a group—a common fear—you might have a nightmare about getting up in front of a crowd and completely forgetting what you were going to say. In Harrison's case, the psychological fear might relate to being small. A nightmare might also be warning you to avoid certain situations or circumstances.

When Todd turned seventeen, he took his birthday cash, combined it with the money he'd saved from his job bagging groceries, and bought his first car. He loved driving his twenty-five-year-old Camaro, and even though it had nearly 200,000 miles on it, he called it a classic, rather than just old. The car payments were taking most of his spare money, but he had managed to save $400 and he was planning on buying a new set of chrome wheels when he had a disturbing dream.

Roller Coaster Ride

I'm racing through town in my car making all the lights. The car feels and looks and sounds exactly like it is. I even notice the medicine wheel that's hanging from my windshield swinging back and forth. I keep going faster and faster. Then, suddenly, the car disappears and I'm riding in a roller coaster whipping around the corners. It's really exhilarating, but then I realize that I'm the only passenger on the roller coaster and it won't stop.

It isn't fun anymore. I'm afraid and I want the ride to end. But I have no control. Then, I hear a big pop, like a loud firecracker, and the roller coaster soars off the track and I'm thrown out. I tumble over and over into the darkness, screaming because I know I'm going to die or get badly injured.

Then I woke up just before I struck the ground. It was so vivid, I felt that it was a warning of some kind, but I didn't know what.

The next morning, Todd thought more about the dream. It really bothered him. Then he remembered that it had begun with him driving his car. The popping sound from the dream made him think of a blowout, the kind that might occur at high speeds on the interstate. He examined his tires and saw that the tread was dangerously thin on his two front tires. He'd been ignoring the condition of the tires because he wanted to get the new chrome wheels. But after the dream, he reluctantly decided to get new tires and hold off on buying the wheels.

Nighttime Notes

While nightmares that warn you of danger sometimes do occur, many nightmares experienced by teens relate to the trials and challenges of growing up.

Although you might become angry or afraid or indignant about the actions of some objectionable character in your dream, the source of your anguish is nearly always something within yourself. The nightmarish situation might reflect some element in yourself that you would rather ignore or keep hidden. For example, the following dream, recorded by a thirteen-year-old girl, might relate a concern about being abandoned.

The Last Light
I'm walking alone, frightened, on a deserted street in the middle of the night. My eyes are twitching, my body is shaking, my heart

is pounding. I wander aimlessly in search of something, anything. Then my walk turns into a sprint as I frantically search for any sign of human life. I notice stores on one side of the street, but they're all empty.

Suddenly, all of the streetlights, except one, blow out and the wind begins to howl. The last light flickers on and off, but manages to stay on.

My heart pounds and my blood races as I hear footsteps. They're getting louder and closer. I panic and run, but there's no place to go. I'm thinking that I'm a goner and fall onto the damp, rough ground. I feel a horrid sting in my neck. The last light flickers one more time and dies. I'm terrified.

I wake up sweating and breathing heavily. My head is spinning. I'm relieved that it was a dream, but it takes about ten minutes before I can fall asleep again.

Nightmares are designed to get our attention. They shock us into acknowledging them and hopefully getting their hidden message, as well. The more vivid and outrageous the nightmare, the easier it is to remember. Even though they make us feel anxious, they can actually be helpful when they're interpreted. That's because they reveal things that are troubling us at a deep level, even though we may not recognize these things in our waking lives. We tend to tell ourselves that everything is fine, that the only problems we have are the ones created by others. Our dreaming self tells us otherwise through the use of these dramatic dreams. Here's a nightmare told by Ali, a thirteen-year-old eighth grader.

Waves on the Beach

I was walking on the beach with my best friend and cousin when the sky turned from blue to purple and the waves got huge. We all ran, but only my cousin and I made it. We climbed up the sand dunes, but then the waves got him, too. I felt upset when I woke up. Even though I knew it was a dream, I was afraid that the waves were going to get me.

While others in the dream are swept away by the high tides of emotion, represented by the waves, Ali maintains self-awareness. The sky is ominous and she's frightened, but she survives. In waking life, she has a strong sense of self. She's determined. Like most middle school students, she is often in the middle of emotional matters relating to friendships, some of which threaten to drag her down. But she knows who she is and moves ahead, even though she still fears getting caught up in the emotional turmoil.

Dissecting a Nightmare

Take a close look at a nightmare, especially if it's a recurring one. In your dream journal, answer the following questions, and use them to dissect your nightmare:

- Where does the dream take place?
- Who are the main characters?
- What are the most significant images?
- Are there any obvious metaphors or puns that stand out?
- How does the dream end?
- If you could confront the forces that oppose you in the dream, how would you rewrite the ending?

Dealing with Nightmares

There's no need to fear your nightmares. Sure, they make you feel uneasy, but it's better to consider them a challenge rather than an obstacle. The characters and incidents may threaten you, but remember that you have the power to overcome the worst enemies, the most vicious monsters, and the most dangerous circumstances.

Keep in mind that we often flee from what we can't control. If you have a recurring nightmare, it probably means that there's a problem in your life that you're avoiding. Dream master Robert Moss calls a nightmare an "aborted dream." That means we fled the dream before its full message was delivered. "Remarkable discoveries await us when we develop the pluck and the skill to return to nightmare scenes to unveil their fuller meaning."

Nighttime Notes

Rather than running or avoiding the problem in your dreams, you can confront your adversary and uncover new things about yourself by taking control of your own nightmare.

If you're having a nightmare about being chased or stalked, here's how to prepare yourself for a confrontation in the dream state. You should try this technique after waking up from a nightmare.

1. Jot down a description of the adversary in your dream journal. Who or what is stalking you?
2. Start a dialogue with your foe. Ask what the stalker wants. This will prepare you for confronting the stalker.
3. Ask yourself why you are running.
4. Is there something about the adversary that reminds you of a part of yourself? If so, what is it?

5. Have you been avoiding a confrontation with this part of yourself that you don't like very much?

If you have trouble answering some of those questions, or if it's hard to relate your nightmare to your waking life, consider what you fear most. What makes you anxious or insecure? Do you feel inadequate in some way? Is it your looks or your intelligence? Does it relate to your future? Do you know what you're going to do after high school? If you're planning on going to college, is there a concern about where you're going or how you're going to pay for it? Or could you be concerned about a relationship with a parent or sibling or friend?

Maybe your nightmare doesn't involve someone chasing you. Instead, you may find yourself in frightening circumstances. Maybe you are losing your teeth, falling from a building, missing a train, or getting lost. You can still apply the same questions about your fears.

Nighttime Notes
When you pinpoint the object of your greatest fear, you might think, "Oh, I can't deal with *that*." But "that" probably is exactly what you need to face.

When I was in my early teens, I had a repeated nightmare about a group of bullies surrounding and threatening me. In every dream, they would catch me behind the school and push me against the wall. Then they would slowly close in and I could feel their anger. I knew I couldn't get away. I felt frightened, unable to react to their taunting words and unable to flee. Just as they were about to pummel me, I would wake up gasping for air.

I could never see their faces, but I suspected the dream had something to do with a gang of kids, two or three years older than I was, who lived in the neighborhood. My friends and I usually tried to stay away from them because we never knew what they would do to us.

I'm not sure how long the nightmares continued, but I remember how they stopped. One night, in the midst of getting cornered, I found my voice in the dream and shouted, "Go to hell, Rollie." That was the name of one of the kids in the gang, the one who picked on me whenever he got a chance. As soon as I shouted, they were gone, and the oppressive feeling lifted. Coincidentally, I never had trouble with Rollie after that. His family moved away!

Confronting Your Dream Adversaries

We talked about the technique for re-entering a dream in Chapter 5. You can use that method to return to a dream and confront whoever or whatever is stalking you. It's best to go back as soon as you can, preferably while you're still in bed. The longer you wait to re-enter a nightmare, the more difficult the task becomes.

You can also confront your foe while the dream is unfolding. To do so, you need to become aware during the nightmare that you are dreaming. (You can find tips on how to "wake up" in a dream—also called lucid dreaming—in Chapter 10.) Then, instead of waking up and fleeing the bad dream, you can turn on whoever is chasing you or whatever situation that exists in the dream and confront your opponent.

Nighttime Notes

There is nothing in a dream that can hurt you. If you question your antagonist, the threat will either disappear completely or become weak and harmless.

The Senoi people of Malaysia, who we talked about in Chapter 6, taught their children to confront whatever was frightening them in their nightmares. This act transforms fear into courage, and a positive outcome is achieved. The next step for the Senoi was to carry dream actions, in one form or another, into waking life. For instance, if a neighbor or acquaintance appeared ill in a dream, the dreamer would go out of his or her way to see how that person was feeling in waking life.

Other Terrors of the Night

You might be surprised to learn that nightmares are not the only fearsome dramas stalking our sleep. Other scary or unpleasant experiences include posttraumatic stress disorder, night terror, and sleep paralysis.

PTSD

If you've undergone a traumatic event, such as surgery, the loss of a loved one, an assault, or a severe accident, you might have experienced posttraumatic stress disorder (PTSD). Unlike other nightmares, the nightmares that follow a severe trauma can involve realistic re-enactments of the traumatic incident. The experiences often are repeated over and over, night after night.

While PTSD isn't unheard of among teens, it tends to happen more frequently to adults. War veterans, in particular, have reported this nighttime affliction. Over time, as you heal from the incident, the nightmares become less realistic and blend with events from other periods of your life. Finally, researchers say, the experiences shift into typical nightmare scenarios involving fantasy figures and incidents that never occurred in your life.

Night Terrors

Night terrors, also known as sleep terror, or *pavor nocturnus*, involves a sudden awakening from sleep and persistent fear or terror. Your heart hammers in your chest. You might scream, sweat profusely, and feel disoriented. Usually the person has no recollection of the incident, only a vague sense of frightening images. Researchers say that many people experiencing night terrors see spiders, snakes, animals, or people in the room.

While nightmares take place during REM sleep—described in Chapter 2—night terrors occurs at a deeper level of sleep, when the brain produces slow delta waves and *no* REM sleep. The night terror experience might last from five to twenty minutes. During that time the person is asleep and unable to wake up, even if his or her eyes are open.

Nighttime Notes

Night terrors can happen to anyone from infants to the elderly.

While it isn't considered dangerous, what you do during the night terror episode can lead into dangerous situations. Some people who experience night terror walk into walls or fall down stairs, which is certainly hazardous.

Here's a description of night terrors provided by a nineteen-year-old named Heather.

One of my most frightening experiences was when I was six years old. I was having the worst night terror of my life. I was sitting in my room, everyone still sleeping, and the walls were falling in around me. The books were all falling off the shelves, walls crashing. I was so scared, but I couldn't do anything. I was in a trance, a haze. My head throbbed and buzzed, and I was sure I would die. From what I'm told, I walked into the living room and turned up the stereo as loud as it could go, and woke up the entire family. I told them about the book shelves falling in my room, and I ranted and raved for about twenty minutes. Some things I said made no sense at all. I was in my own world, more like my own hell. Finally, my mother put me in a cold bath and I "sobered up." That was one of the most traumatic experiences of my life and one that I will never be able to forget. Even now when I think about it, I get shivers down my spine.

Heather reported her experience on the online Night Terror Resource Center, at *www.nightterrors.org*. She said that her night terrors stopped when she turned twelve, and she considers herself very lucky.

Sleep Paralysis

Have you ever awakened from a dream or nightmare and realized that you couldn't move or cry out, but you were able to see or sense the presence of some unknown being? This frightening experience is known as sleep paralysis. It is sometimes accompanied by terrifying hypnagogic images—those surreal scenes you see when you're halfway between sleep and waking—that flit through your mind like scenes from a horror movie.

The visions usually generate a feeling of dread, as if someone or something evil is lurking nearby. These experiences can last between thirty seconds and seven or eight minutes. Sometimes sleep paralysis is brought on by stress or a lack of sleep. Like night terrors, the experience itself isn't considered dangerous.

Nighttime Notes

Sleep paralysis differs from night terrors in that the episodes occur in the first stage of sleep when you are usually on the border between wakefulness and sleep.

A frequent hallucination during sleep paralysis is the sensation of a small creature sitting on the sleeper's chest. The creature either compresses the chest or attempts to strangle the sleeper. Invariably, those reporting such attacks have been sleeping on their backs.

It's interesting to note that different cultures throughout history have related these experiences to varying forms of spirit contact. In Southeast Asia, the creature that appears during sleep paralysis is considered an ancestral ghost. In Irish and Scottish traditions, it's a hag. The Chinese see the beings as cats, while the Japanese consider them ghostly foxes. In Arabic countries, they're called *djinn*; in Mexico, they're known as *brujos,* or witches. The ancient Romans and Egyptians related them to feelings of guilt, while in medieval Europe they were called demons and later vampires.

Today, in America and in many other countries, people who say they have been visited or abducted by aliens describe sleep paralysis symptoms. They feel as if they are awake but unable to move or shout, and they see small beings controlling them. Sometimes, they experience a sensation of being floated into an alien craft. A spooky question arises from such episodes. Are alien abduction scenarios simply another way of experiencing sleep paralysis, or is sleep paralysis a symptom of alien abductions?

In spite of the frightening experiences, some people make an effort to stay alert and aware during sleep paralysis. In doing so, they feel that they can resist abduction by aliens. Staying conscious also presents the opportunity for the dreamer to explore other realms through out-of-body experiences and lucid dreams, the subject of the next chapter.

Alien

The hidden or unrevealed parts of your being may appear as an alien. An alien could also represent a shadow or negative side of yourself. How does it relate to you? What is your reaction? Does the being appear more evolved or monstrous? What part of you is like the alien?

Ten

The Freaky Side of Dreaming

Only the dreamer can change the dream.
—JOHN LOGAN, SCOTTISH POET

What if there is much more to the world than what we realize? What if whole realms exist just beyond our vision, and what if we can have real abilities in our dreams that go way beyond what's possible in waking life?

If you can accept such possibilities, then you're ready to journey to the far side of dreaming. This is the place where dreamers wake up inside their own dreams; where you can leave your body to spy on your friends or visit other worlds; a place where you even can contact the dead and get in touch with spirit guides.

Lucid Dreaming

The word "lucid" is normally used to describe thoughts that are clear, easy to understand, and rational. To be lucid in a dream means that your conscious, or rational, mind is aware you are dreaming. Knowing you are dreaming sometimes gives you the power to change events within the dream. The sensation is exhilarating and memorable, even if the experience only lasts a few seconds. In the lucid state, you can do things that defy normal reality. You can fly, walk through a wall, or dance on the ceiling.

Sometimes it is the spontaneous, usually joyous, dream experiences—like dream flying—that trigger your lucid dreaming experience. Other times, it might be some strange aspect of the dream landscape that gets your attention. Or you might come awake within a dream at the sound of some powerful, inspiring music or simply a voice in your ear telling you to look around.

Nighttime Notes

It is a big accom-plishment to awaken—or become lucid—inside a dream, whether it happens all by itself or because you made it happen.

Sleep researcher Stephen LaBerge, who has written two excellent books on lucid dreaming, began his first book with one of his own lucid dreams. In the dream, LaBerge finds himself in a magnificent castle. "As I wandered through a high-vaulted corridor deep within a mighty citadel, I paused to admire the magnificent architecture. Somehow the contemplation of these majestic surroundings stimulated the realization that I was *dreaming!* In the light of my lucid consciousness, the already impressive splendor of the castle appeared even more of a marvel, and with great excitement I began to explore the imaginary reality of my 'castle in the air.'"

To explain his state of mind, LaBerge added, "Fantastic as it may sound, I was in full possession of my waking faculties while dreaming and soundly asleep: I could think as clearly as ever, freely remember details of my waking life, and act deliberately upon conscious reflection."

Usually people experience a lucid dream spontaneously before they attempt to create the experience. If you're not sure whether or not you've had a lucid dream, then you probably haven't. When you do, you'll definitely know it. If you have never found yourself fully awake in a dream, you can try one or both of the methods presented here. It may not be easy to enter a lucid dream state, but it's definitely worth the effort.

Nighttime Notes

Although scientists didn't begin seriously studying lucid dreaming until the 1970s, the practice of conscious dreaming has been around for centuries. Back in the eighth century, a Tibetan yoga master wrote about dreaming while fully conscious in a book called *Yoga and the Dream State*. A couple of centuries later, another Tibetan master, Atisha, wrote about being simultaneously awake and asleep in *The Seven Points of Mind Training*.

Entering a Lucid Dream

You might find an opportunity to enter a lucid dream just as you are beginning to fall asleep. As you get drowsy and drift into the first stage of sleep, you'll see a rapid series of images flashing in front of your mind's eye. You may recall from Chapter 2 that these surreal scenes are known as hypnagogic images. In this state of light sleep, you are still awake. Your goal is to hang onto this small degree of wakefulness in order to experience a lucid dream.

Staying Focused

Dream researcher Robert Moss suggests focusing on a single image or scene and holding it as if you were cradling a newborn child. Gradually, you will be led into a full-fledged dream, and the challenge will be to remain awake and conscious. Now you'll have the opportunity to experiment with this awake-but-dreaming reality. It's the perfect chance to fly. Just suggest that you are ready to take off and select a target, maybe a friend's house.

In my flying dreams, I usually take a few steps, each one getting longer and longer until I'm airborne. Don't panic or get too excited if you start moving fast; that might cause you to slide into a regular dream or lose your conscious awareness. Just go with the flow of the dream, but keep reminding yourself that you are dreaming.

The LaBerge Way

Stephen LaBerge prefers another method for entering a lucid dream. For his method to work, you remember and record your dreams in your dream journal on a regular basis. Look back over your old entries and hunt for "dream signs." That's the term LaBerge uses to describe odd dream experiences, which might indicate that you are ready to try lucid dreaming. I recall one distinctive dream sign I encountered: a twenty-foot-long stalk of celery, which I casually carried home.

Dream Signs

After looking over your dream journal, jot down any dream signs that you think you've found. In which of the four categories below does your dream sign fit?

1. Dream characters, including friends, who transform themselves into other people or other creatures.
2. Strong emotions or intense sensations, such as expanded vision or incredible hearing.
3. Experiencing unusual or impossible abilities, such as walking on water or diving inside the earth.
4. Unusual experiences of time and space, such as finding yourself on another planet, soaring toward the moon, or realizing that you were dreaming of another time in the past or future.

If you've recorded some of your dream signs and can easily identify them, you're ready to try the lucid dreaming exercise in "Looking for Dream Signs."

Keep in mind that if you need to get up early for school, you might want to limit your attempts at lucid dreaming to the weekend.

Looking for Dream Signs

1. When you wake up from a dream, especially early in the morning, think about the details of the dream. Look for dream signs. Go over the dream a few times in your mind. Memorize it.

2. While you're still in bed, spend ten or fifteen minutes writing in or reading your dream journal. If it's still dark, turn on a light so you stay fully awake. If you share a bedroom, you might go into another room to read or write and come back when you're ready to go back to sleep.

3. Go back to bed. Focus your intention on entering a dream while recognizing that you're dreaming. Think of something you'd like to do in this dream. For example, you might want to fly or to go visit a friend.

4. Next, imagine that you're asleep. See yourself in the dream you just memorized. Tell yourself that you are dreaming. Say to yourself, "One, I'm dreaming. Two, I'm dreaming," and so on. At some point, as you repeat the phrase, you will actually begin to dream. As images come to you, look for a dream sign. Hold the image and realize that you are awake and dreaming. Now you can pursue the goal you set out for yourself in your dream.

You may have to try this method a couple of times before you succeed. When you do succeed, your first lucid dreams may be very short. It is startling and thrilling to realize while you're dreaming that you're also awake and able to consciously affect a dream experience. Until you learn how to control your reaction, you might wake you up after a few seconds and lose your hold on the dream.

If you're interested in learning more about the subject, take a look at one of the books by Stephen LaBerge on the subject, either *Lucid Dreaming: The Power of Being Awake and Aware in Your Dreams* or *Exploring the World of Lucid Dreaming*.

Lucid dreaming isn't easy, and your first attempts might not be completely successful. Even so, they *will* be memorable. For days after, whenever you think about what you managed to do, you'll get a kick out of remembering your accomplishment.

Robert Moss, in his book *Conscious Dreaming*, notes that many dreamers are startled into a lucid state by auditory signals within their dreams, such as a ringing telephone or doorbell, a siren, or a voice. He recalls a dream in which he became lucid upon hearing a voice: "A companion I had not previously noticed asked me, 'Where is your body?'—making me aware that I was dreaming and that I was outside my body."

So was Moss having a lucid dream or an out-of-body experience? As you'll see in the next section, the two phenomena are closely linked. In both cases, the subject is fully aware that he or she is dreaming, and both are usually short-lived experiences. (Unless, that is, you have learned to control the awesome state of being awake within a dream.)

Out-of-Body Experiences

Out-of-body experiences, also known as "OBEs," occur when your consciousness seems to depart from your body. This change in perspective enables you to observe the world from a point of view outside your physical body. Most out-of-body experiences are fleeting. When people realize that their awareness is suddenly separate from their bodies, they are usually shocked out of the experience and back to their physical bodies. With practice, it is possible to overcome the fear.

Nighttime Notes

While out-of-body travel is an adventurous undertaking, you don't have to worry about getting lost. You belong in your body and will certainly find your way back.

In a sense, OBEs are just a different way of thinking about lucid dreams. However, there are some differences. While the scenes, characters, and actions within a lucid dream are usually surreal, out-of-body travelers often report scenes that look and feel like the waking world. In some cases, they can accurately describe people and objects they saw during their experience. Some have even reported overhearing conversations that actually took place.

In OBEs, the dreamer feels separated from his or her physical body, but there is also an identification with a dream body. Many people have reported hovering above their beds and seeing their sleeping bodies. But an OBE also can take dreamers far from home.

Nighttime Notes

Out-of-body travelers have reported trips to the past or future, other worlds, and other dimensions. They also have described contact with spirits of the dead.

136

One of the most noted out-of-body explorers was a Virginia businessman named Robert Monroe, who began spontaneously traveling out of his body while in a relaxed state at the edge of sleep. At first, he thought he was going crazy, but after numerous medical tests proved negative, he decided to begin researching the places he ventured in the out-of-body state. His pioneering adventures allowed him to explore our own world as well as other realms, including the astral plane. There, he visited spirits of the dead and nonhuman beings of superior intelligence. He also slipped into a parallel world similar to our own, yet with distinct differences, and he ventured into levels of existence that are beyond our understanding. Ultimately, he wrote *Journeys Out of Body* and two other books on his experiences. In his latter years, he founded the Monroe Institute, which is dedicated to exploring the out-of-body experience.

Attempting an Out-of-Body Experience

Monroe believed that we all have frequent out-of-body experiences while sleeping, but conscious OBEs are rare occurrences. You can increase the odds of having an OBE by programming yourself to enter such a dream. Monroe found that the best time to prepare for an out-of-body experience is at the very edge of sleep, while the mind is still alert but those surreal, hypnagogic images are starting to form. Here is the method he recommended.

Relax

1. Find a comfortable place where you won't be interrupted. Begin by entering a relaxed state.
2. Take long, deep breaths, feeling yourself relaxing more and more on each exhalation.

3. Then, as your breath becomes gentle, imagine a wave of relaxation rippling down your body all the way to your feet. The goal is to reach that drowsy state between wakefulness and sleep and to maintain it without falling asleep.

4. Focus on something such as an image, a word, or even your breath. When you can maintain your hold on this borderland state without falling asleep, you've passed the first step.

5. Next, try to hold that borderland state without concentrating on anything. Just focus on the blackness in front of you. Eliminate any nervousness or unease you might feel. In the last part of the relaxation process, you should release your hold on the borderland sleep and start to slowly drift deeper while still remaining conscious. Give yourself a suggestion. Say to yourself, "I will remember everything I experience that is good for my physical and mental being." Repeat this thought several times.

Create Vibrations

The second step involves creating vibrations in the body.

1. Monroe suggests that you can set up the vibrational waves by imagining two lines that extend forward along the sides of your head and meet about a foot in front of your eyes. Think of these lines as charged wires that are joined or as opposite poles of a magnet that are connected.

2. Once they converge, imagine that point moving farther out in front of you, three feet out, then six feet.

3. Imagine that the lines are rotating, so that instead of pointing out in front of you, they extend up above your head.

4. With your mind, reach through the top of your head to the point where the lines meet.

5. Keep reaching until you feel a reaction. This might be a hissing or roaring sound in your head that spreads through your body, surging and ebbing in a rhythmic manner like the flow of the tide.

Release the Fear

When attempting an OBE, fear is the biggest obstacle you will face. It's important to eliminate any sense of worry or panic.

The first time the vibrations occur, you might feel like you're being electrocuted, even though there is no pain involved. Once you get used to the vibrations, use your mind to direct them to form a ring that sweeps around your body, from head to toe and back again. Once you've got the momentum going, let it proceed on its own. The faster and smoother the vibration, the easier it is to separate.

Control Your Thoughts

Focus on a single thought, such as "float upward," or a specific location you want to reach. Remain focused and calm, not allowing any fear to enter your mind.

Separation and Liftoff

Imagine yourself floating upward. Think about how wonderful the sensation will be. Imagine yourself getting lighter and lighter. If you hold these thoughts, you'll lift off. You can also rotate your way out—turn over—just as you would if you were trying to get more comfortable in bed.

Out-of-Body Skeptics

If you're skeptical about that possibility that anyone can leave their body and travel while remaining conscious, you're not alone. But as a result of extensive research, the phenomenon has gained increased acceptance among scientists. Dr. Michael Sabom, a cardiologist and author of the book *Recollections of Death,* studied people who were medically dead for short periods of time and then returned to life. Many described OBEs in which they watched medical personnel try to save them. They often provided accurate details of things they shouldn't have known about, such as surgical procedures and the medical personnel involved. Since Sabom had access to medical records and personnel, he was able to verify their observations.

Nighttime Notes
Until recent years, many scientists believed OBEs were simply hallucinations.

Shamanism

Imagine if you could come awake in a dream, become a bird, and fly away! Shamans, considered the "medicine people" of native cultures, do just that. In many cultures, shamans practice conscious dreaming, combining out-of-body experiences with shape-shifting. During their experiences they often encounter "guardian" beings, which sometimes take human form and other times appear as animals or other beings. Although shamanism is linked to the past and to primitive cultures, the ancient practice is alive today both in indigenous cultures and through a new age of shamans, many of them raised and educated in the Western world. Some of these Western shamans have been trained by elders, who are part of a native culture or who have links to one.

Although there is considerable confusion on what shamans do, dreaming is at the heart of their practice. They gain insight and healing abilities through dreams, which they then use to help others.

Nighttime Notes

Shamans have developed the ability to enter the dream world at will to communicate with dream guides, to journey across time and space, and to enter into other realms.

In indigenous cultures, a shaman often learns of his calling in a dream, known as the "big dream," and much of his work involves guidance in the dream world. Such guidance comes from communication with guardian spirits or a power animal. "A big dream is one that is repeated several times in the same basic way on different nights, or it is a one-time dream that is so vivid that it is like being awake," says Michael Harner, an anthropologist who has practiced shamanism for three decades.

The difference between a shamanic dream, or big dream, and a lucid dream, or OBE, is that the shamanic dream deals with spirit guidance and the intent of gaining power or knowledge. A lucid dream or OBE, on the other hand, is a nonphysical adventure, a journey that's not necessarily linked with any spiritual tradition or related goal.

Harner and his colleagues have held hundreds of workshops on shamanism in which they teach skills handed down over the millennia. "In my shamanic workshops, these new practitioners are not 'playing Indian,' but going to the same revelatory spiritual sources that tribal shamans have traveled to from time immemorial . . . Their experiences are genuine and, when described, are essentially interchangeable with the accounts of shamans from nonliterate tribal cultures." Often these encounters with guardian spirits include training sessions in the dream state.

But you don't have to be a shaman-in-training to experience out-of-body adventures with the company of a guardian being. Sometimes they occur spontaneously, and such guardians can assume a variety of identities. Take this dream, recorded by twelve-year-old JoAnna.

Flying with an Owl

I was walking alone outside in the dark, but I wasn't afraid. I could see everything around me, almost as if it were daylight. Then I heard a hoot from a tree. I looked up and then I was in the air next to a branch. I saw an owl's yellow eyes blinking at me. Then it lifted off from the branch and flew away and I was flying with it. I don't know how I could fly, but it was easy and I felt safe with the owl. It protected me and it told me things that were important. But when I woke up, I couldn't remember anything it said. But I felt really good. I knew it was an important dream.

JoAnna's parents have supported her dream work since she was young and encouraged her to explore spiritual realms in nontraditional ways. Her dream suggests that she was being guided into other worlds and higher knowledge. With its ability to see in the dark, the owl is associated with wisdom and higher perception. It represents both knowledge and mystery and is a symbol of the unconscious mind, the realm of the dreaming self.

Power Objects

One means of entering a shamanic dream involves the use of power objects. These objects are usually passed down from shaman to shaman over the generations. They might be carved stone figures, bead necklaces, crystals, engraved metal pieces, or even rattles. A shaman might select a power object and keep it nearby before going to sleep. Through the object, the shaman might obtain a power dream.

I experienced a memorable power dream using this method a few years ago in Canyon de Chelly on the Navajo reservation. I was part of a group who were trekking the canyon with Alberto Villoldo, a medical anthropologist and shaman associated with the Q'ero Indians, who live high in the Andes. The Q'eros, whose villages are located at altitudes more than 14,000 feet above sea level, are considered direct descendants of the Incas. One evening, as we gathered in a large tent, Villoldo took out his *mesa,* a cloth bag containing power objects that had been given to him by shamans of his lineage.

The power objects were passed around our circle, and we handled each one without looking at them. Then we selected the one that appealed most to us. That night we were to sleep with the object nearby in the hopes of obtaining a power dream.

Nighttime Notes

Power objects can be passed through generations and can be anything at all—carved stone figures, bead necklaces, crystals. What would your power object be?

Several of us, in fact, experienced dreams that seemed to relate directly to the object we had selected. Rachel, a mother of three, dreamed of seeing mountains around her. Somehow, she knew she was in South America. She didn't understand why she was seeing another place, since we were in the Southwest. Then she glimpsed a black panther. "It came right into my forehead through a physical opening. Everything opened up then and I had a sense of being in a primordial lost paradise of the Native Americans. I sensed the people and the earth."

Rachel's power object was a small, smooth stone wrapped in a rough piece of cloth. Villoldo told her he wasn't surprised that she'd seen South American mountains and experienced the cat entering her forehead. The stone had been given to him by the high shaman of the Q'eros, the equivalent of the Dalai Lama.

That same night, I dreamed of seeing myself dressed and packed for a journey. I was on a train, and floating directly above me was a woman, who I knew was also me. Then there was my dreaming self, who was observing the other two on the journey.

The next morning, after I related my dream, Villoldo told me that the smooth, three-pronged stone that I'd selected was associated with the three worlds of the Incas: the *Kaypacha,* the physical world; the *Ukhupacha,* the inner world or dreaming world; and *Hanaqpacha,* the higher world. "We all have multiple selves living simultaneously in each of these worlds." My dream had portrayed aspects of myself from each of these worlds.

Nighttime Notes
You may have a power object already, without even knowing it.

Entering a Power Dream

You don't necessarily need a shaman to guide you, or even a power object from an ancient lineage of shamans, to enter a power dream. You may have a power object in your possession without even knowing it.

Such an object might be a family heirloom that has been passed down from generation to generation. Maybe it's a necklace or a wedding band that belonged to your grandmother that had once belonged to her mother or grandmother. The idea is that such an object possesses "stored memories" or messages that you can reach through dreaming.

Preparing Your Power Object

First, you need to prepare your power object.

1. Hold it in your hand awhile before going to bed for the night. Quiet your mind, and focus on the object. It doesn't matter if you don't know much about it. In fact, it's better if you don't know the object's history. That way your dream definitely won't be based on memories but on psychic impressions.

2. Pay attention to any preliminary impressions. If you don't feel good about the object for some reason, you may want to find something else.

3. After a few minutes, put the object under your pillow.

4. As you start to get drowsy, tell yourself that you want to receive a dream of power from someone once associated with the object.

5. Add that only a positive experience will result and your life will be empowered by it.

6. In the morning, or whenever you awaken from your dream, jot it down in your journal. Make sure you note that you incubated a power dream. Write down your thoughts about the object as well as your dream. When you interpret the dream, describe your link to the object.

7. If the object once belonged to someone who is now dead, your dream might be a form of communication with that person. You may be surprised to know that dreams of contact with the dead are quite common, especially in the first year or two after the person's death.

Dream Contact with the Dead

Meeting dead people in your dreams might sound scary, but usually it's not. In fact, the dead typically seem very alive in the dream state. I've encountered the dead in my dreams. In one particular instance, my cousin John appeared to me. He was smiling and looked healthy. He seemed happy to see me, but somewhat confused. "What's going on?" he asked.

His appearance surprised me because in waking life I knew that John did not look well at all. He had brain cancer, was in a coma, and was expected to die. Did my dream indicate that he would recover? Two days later, I received word of his death. His appearance to me—in particular, the *way* he looked when he appeared—was a message. He was in a coma, his body failing, yet his spirit was alive and well. He was about to move on.

Rosemary Ellen Guiley, author of *Dreamwork for the Soul,* tells of a dreamer who was obsessed with the question of what happens at death. He didn't want to believe that existence ended with death, but he saw no logical alternative and it angered him. Finally, he had a dream in which a voice asked if he wanted to find out what it's like to die. Abruptly, he heard a loud crack of thunder and found himself traveling rapidly through a tunnel, passing through arcs of light. Then the tunnel ended, and he

Nighttime Notes

Besides containing messages from the dead, dreams can also give you insight into the afterlife.

was sitting on a bench in a park. He saw other people walking through the park and heard birds singing. If this was what it was like to die, it wasn't so bad, he thought. Instantly, he woke up in bed. He felt pleased with the experience and stopped fretting about death.

Robert Monroe described a similar parklike setting in *Journeys Out of Body.* He calls it a postdeath way station where incoming souls can relax, rest, and meet with deceased friends and relatives and with guides. He described some of the people in the park as dazed or disoriented, while others were calm. "Somehow I knew that this was a meeting place, where the newly arrived waited for friends or relatives. From this Place of Meeting, these friends would take each newcomer to the proper place where he or she 'belonged.'"

Nighttime Notes

Dreams of contact with the deceased and dreams of the afterlife might show you that life continues after death. They not only can provide you personal confirmation of the reality of the soul, but give you glimpses of the possible destinations awaiting you in the afterlife.

An encounter with someone who has died makes for one of the most important dreams we can experience. Such dream messages are intended to bring closure for a grieving loved one, sometimes through an intermediary, or middle man. From time to time, I seem to serve as an intermediary between the dead and their loved ones. I've had numerous dreams of contact with the recently deceased and the message is always clear: We live on. Although I enjoy these dream encounters, feel uplifted by them, and usually gain knowledge and understanding, being an intermediary is not always a position that I relish. Essentially, I'm placing myself between the living spouse and the dead loved one. Sometimes the grieving survivor wants to know why the deceased spouse would contact me instead of him or her.

In one case, I waited weeks to pass a message along. I'd already given a message to this surviving spouse, who seemed skeptical and less than appreciative and I didn't think that she wanted to hear any more. But one day my thirteen-year-old daughter gave me a nudge, telling me to call the wife of my old friend and give her the message. I hesitated, but to my surprise, she called me later the same day on an unrelated matter. This time she accepted the message graciously and with interest. She was open not only to the message but also to the reality of the contact.

A dream message can also provide guidance. Robert Moss recounts the story of a teenage boy who was having trouble in school when he dreamed his deceased grandfather appeared to him and gave him a vision of his future. He saw himself in his mid twenties, wearing a tuxedo, about to marry a beautiful young woman. The grandfather shared more details about the boy's future, but the rest of it was forgotten by the time he woke up. The dream gave him the knowledge he needed to move ahead with his life and away from the problems he was facing.

Mail

A message is on the way. Someone might be trying to contact you. Alternately, your unconscious might be sending you a message. It may relate to your need to communicate with others and make sure they get your message.

Eleven

The Power of Dreaming

If the dream is a translation of waking life, waking life is also a translation of the dream.

—RENE MAGRITTE, BELGIAN ARTIST

Imagine that you are thinking about a friend named Claire, whom you haven't seen since fourth grade. You wonder for a second what happened to her, and then you don't think any more about it. But later that day, you get a call—it's Claire! She has just moved back to town after living in another city for five years. "It's great to hear from you," you say. "You're not going to believe this, but I was just thinking about you today."

Or say your mother is asking a lot of personal questions about you and your friends, maybe while you're trying to watch television. She's getting too nosy, and you say, "Mom, that's none of your business." At that moment, one of the television characters says, "Yeah, that's none of your business"—just as though the character knew what was going on in your room and was confirming your judgment.

Are these examples of coincidence, things of no significance whatsoever? Definitely not, said Carl Jung. He called these unlikely collisions of unrelated, but similar events examples of "synchronicity." They are reminders that a subtle dreamlike quality underlies our waking life.

Nighttime Notes

Synchronicity may seem like a big word, but its meaning is simple: your dream life and your waking life may be more related than you think!

Waking Life as a Dream

In this chapter, you'll see that what you've learned about dreams and their interpretations can be applied to your daily life. Synchronicity is one reminder of the connection between the dream world and waking life. Examples of synchronicity are like road signs put up by our unconscious minds to point out certain patterns developing in our lives. As we become aware of synchronicity, we notice it happening more and more.

Nighttime Notes

If you can step back from the dramas in your waking life and think of them as dreams, you can use your dream interpretation skills to help you understand what happens to you while you're awake as well as while you're dreaming.

Interpreting life as a dream can give you a new perspective on your life. Consider this story related by Lynn, a high school senior, who was getting ready for college when things started going wrong.

Although the college of her choice had accepted her, her parents decided that the out-of-state tuition was too expensive. She hoped they would change their minds and as a result missed the deadline for applying to the nearby state university. Now she didn't know what she was going to do.

The same day that she realized her dilemma, she lost her watch. For the next three days, she went about her business without being able to check the time. Although not having her watch was an annoyance, she realized that she could get by pretty easily without one.

Soon she was confronted by more incidents related to time. The day after she lost her watch, the bus she took to school was ten minutes late, then the basketball game after school started half an hour late, because the visiting team was tardy. To top it off, her mother got stuck in traffic, and Lynn had to wait longer than expected for a ride home. They were all minor inconveniences, she noted, and in the end it didn't really matter. She made it to her first class in time, the basketball game was played, and she arrived home just in time for dinner.

On the third day, she found her watch in the bottom of her purse. That same day, she got a message from the college registration office at the state university that an application extension was available. Suddenly, she knew she would get into college. The loss of the watch and the series of missed deadlines reflected Lynn's apparent loss of access to college, which she thought was related to "bad timing." However, the message that her unconscious mind was sending her was that the tardiness wouldn't matter and, as she soon found out, that was true.

The Naskapi Way

In many primitive cultures, the distinction between dreams and waking life was much less defined than it is today in the Western world. The dream life and the waking life were closely related and even flowed together. The Naskapi are an example of one such culture, which lives on today.

The Naskapi Indians inhabit an inhospitable region of northeastern Canada. There are about 800 members of the tribe, which has no government or institutions and no organized religion. Life is centered upon the hunt for caribou and bear and on the tribe's rich spiritual environment.

"Central to the life of the Naskapi," writes David Peat in *Synchronicity*, "is the Big Dream, in which the hunter goes on the trail, meets friends, and locates herds of caribou." Once the hunter wakes from the dream, he will quite often start drumming and chanting to communicate the dream to those around him. In this way, the spirits of the animals in the bush are alerted to the dream.

Nighttime Notes

According to the beliefs of the Naskapi, a hunter's dreams will become clearer and more powerful if he respects the animals and other members of his tribe. If he violates this code of respect, his dreams will desert him.

In conjunction with dreams, the Naskapi also use various forms of divination, or fortune-telling, including a bone oracle. The greatest diviners in the tribe are those who are in deepest harmony with the Manitou, or spirit of the animals. After tossing a bone into a fire, they study the cracks and dark spots for information on everything from trails to the location of herds.

The survival of the tribe depends on each hunter's ability "to recognize patterns and the flux of nature and to live in harmony with them," Peat notes.

Find the Patterns, Make the Connection

Although your life is probably very different than the life of the Naskapi people, you can also learn to recognize and understand patterns in your life and in your dreams. Think about the events in your current life. Try to think of your life as a dream, and interpret the events in it using the same techniques you learned in the earlier chapters.

Try interviewing yourself to uncover the meaning of the events. Be alert for symbols or significant images or words. Consider the events in your life in the same way you would think about the elements of a recurring dream.

- Are there any dramas in your life that are repeated over and over?
- Do you have trouble getting along with your schoolmates or friends, with teachers or your parents?
- Do you do well in school, or do you get in trouble and receive poor grades?
- Do things happen in your life that make you feel good about your future, or do you feel that there is little hope? If so, why?
- Is your health good, or do you get sick a lot?

Reading the Messages

All of the dramas and incidents in your life can be looked at as patterns, your internal life made visible in your external life. In other words, these patterns in your life are messages from your unconscious mind that are communicated through daily dramas. By learning to recognize, interpret, and work with the patterns that operate in your life, you can become better able to control and shape your destiny.

Really what you are doing here is creating an affirmation, that is, a powerful statement about a condition that doesn't exist yet but that you would like to make happen in your life. You can work with these new statements—and make them into new life *patterns*—in your dreams by using them as suggestions before going to sleep.

- Recognize the patterns, especially the ones that you want to get rid of.
- Rewrite your life. For example, let's say that you answered one of the questions above with the comment, "My health is always breaking down. Every time I get well, I just get sick again.

- Now, rewrite the comment this way: "My health is excellent. I rarely get ill." Likewise, if you wrote: "I have trouble getting along with certain people in my life," you could rewrite that statement to say, "I get along well with my friends, and family, and others."

As you already know, your dreams are powerful, wonderful things. By learning to interpret and even create your dreams, you are also learning to understand your life and make it better.

Dream Glossary

A

actor:

Seeing yourself as an actor in the spotlight suggests a desire for publicity or recognition, a role in public life. Such a dream can also imply that you're acting out a role or "putting on an act" for someone. If you're playing the same role over and over again in the same dream or in repeating dreams, it might suggest that you are stuck and not moving forward. Look for fitting metaphors. Do you need to "act your age"? Are you "acting like a fool," or do you need to "get your act together"? If you are acting in a school play, such a dream simply might be a way of processing the day's events.

airplane:

Taking off on a new journey. Depending on what happens, the flight can relate to your hopes and anxieties. Are you soaring high, trying to "stay above it all," or are you "taking flight"?

airport:

A point of transition, moving from one condition to another. Suggests a life change, such as moving from one school to another or graduating. Also carries a sense of movement, activity, going places. Finding yourself in an airport could mean the end of something, as in "terminal." Alternately, there might be a new opportunity, something different, especially if you're standing by a gate. Look at the other aspects of the dream. Are you arriving or leaving? Have you lost your luggage? (If so, look up the word "luggage" for further clarification.)

alien:

The hidden or unrevealed parts of your being may appear as an alien. An alien could also represent a shadow or negative side of yourself. How does it relate to you? What is your reaction? Does the being appear more evolved or monstrous? What part of you is like the alien? Alternately, contact with the unknown could relate to an exploration of the mysterious and of the unconscious. Increasingly, aliens are seen as visitors from another dimension rather than outer space.

animals:

In general, animals often relate to our emotions as well as our sense of creativity.

alligator:

Hidden instincts, potential danger. Could relate to a concern about being attacked or assaulted, either from within yourself or from a powerful figure in your life. Alternately, especially if the alligator is passive, might suggest that you are being thick-skinned or insensitive toward someone. According to Carl Jung, the more primitive the animal, the deeper its sources in the unconscious.

bear:

Could relate to cyclical matters, since bears hibernate. A new awakening. Also fertility and the unconscious, vitality and strength. In Greek mythology, bears represent mothering, but in Native American lore, the bear is the father or grandfather possessing wisdom and sacred knowledge. The image can also be a pun for the need for exposure in some aspect of your life. Your dreaming self might be telling you that you need to open up to others, as in "baring your soul." Also a danger, a threat, as in something "bearing down" on you. In folklore, bears often represent female, motherly energy, and bearskins are associated with protective magical powers. Other metaphors and puns include a bear market, when the stock market declines; or patience, as in "bear with me"; finding a path, that is "getting your bearings"; and tough personal relationships, or dealing with an "overbearing" person.

bird:

The appearance of a bird could relate to a wish for freedom, to fly away. A caged bird represents a feeling of being trapped. Birds can also be spiritual symbols. Among certain Native American tribes, an eagle symbolizes spiritual knowledge. A hawk is far-sighted, aggressive, on the hunt. It's a predator that attacks other birds and steals from their nests. Are you hunting for something, or are you concerned about the loss of something? A soaring hawk in a dream might suggest the need for insight. It also might mean that the dreamer should keep a "hawk's eye" on someone or a situation. A vulture might symbolize death, while a hummingbird suggests a tendency to flit from one thing to another (and, alternately, that things are humming along). A penguin—a black-and-white, flightless bird living in frigid conditions—represents stiff formality, a feeling of being grounded or getting a frosty reception. A peacock represents boasting and pride. A turkey might represent a feast or family gathering, but a turkey is also a dud. A flock

of birds can represent mystery or danger, as in the famous Alfred Hitchcock movie, *The Birds.*

bull:

Aggressive, "bullish" behavior, stubborn, a lack of truthfulness, as in "full of bull." Bragging, as in "shooting the bull." Also incorrect information, as in "getting a bum steer." In astrology, the bull relates to Taurus, an earth sign, which is about being persistent, determined, and stable.

cat:

The emotional, intuitive, or magical, the unconscious willpower. Cats can have both positive and negative connotations, depending on your association with cats and the surrounding circumstances in the dream. Cats can mean prosperity; kittens can mean new ideas. Kittens in a basement could be ideas arising from the unconscious mind. Cats can represent independence, the feminine mystique. They can also stand for evil or bad luck, or a catty or cunning person. For either a man or woman, the dream of a cat relates to the anima, the feminine nature of the personality.

dog:

Devotion, loyalty, a true friend. Also instinct, emotions. On the negative side, the metaphor could be "He follows me around like a dog." A guard dog might relate to protecting property.

goat:

Ability to survive difficulties, sure-footed, scrappy, symbolic of a social climber. Also associated with repressed drives, the underworld, and evil. A goat also is a symbol of the devil, a link probably derived from Pan, a Greek pagan god, who was part goat and part man. In astrology, associated with Capricorn, an earth sign related to structure, self-discipline, and ambition.

horse:

A horse symbolizes strength, power, endurance, majesty, and virility. A boy dreaming of a horse might desire manhood; a woman might be expressing a desire for intimacy. Riding a horse suggests one is in a powerful position. White horses represent purity, while black horses represent a postponement of pleasure. If you work with horses or regularly ride, the dream simply might be a processing of the day's events without significant symbolic meaning.

lion:

A driving force, sense of power, victory. If the lion is chasing you, the indication is that you are vulnerable to attack. A caged lion implies that you will be successful as long as the opposition is held in check. Alternately, a lion can represent a male authority figure, someone you look up to or fear. In astrology, Leo the lion is a fire sign, a symbol of courage, confidence, recognition, and personal magnetism.

owl:

Wisdom, higher perception, vision in the dark. It represents both wisdom and mystery and is a symbol of the unconscious. In folklore, owls are seen as warning signs of death.

oxen:

Great strength, endurance, an ability to carry on against all odds. Alternately, work that is never-ending, a sense of being burdened. Alternately, it could suggest that you are a burden to others.

pig:

Greed, lack of discipline, sloppy habits. A despicable person, a "swine." A stubborn person, "pigheaded." In spite of the numerous metaphors equating pigs with degrading behavior, pigs are instinctive and deceptively smart. In folklore, the pig represents the womb, fertility.

ram:

Masculine energy, aggressiveness. The power of renewal, head of the flock. Also making your case in an overly aggressive manner, as in "ramming your point home." Are you pushing so hard in some area of your life that you are acting like a "battering ram"? In astrology, the ram relates to Aries, a fire sign, which is about initiative, willpower, and strength.

rat:

Underhanded activities, fear or anxiety, a negative part of oneself. Are you or someone else acting like a rat? Do you "smell a rat"? Also turning against someone, as in "ratting on him." Are you feeling trapped, like a "cornered rat"? But a dream related to a pet rat expresses more appealing sentiments, such as intelligence, vulnerability, instinct, caring.

tiger:

Aggressive and cunning behavior, power. Are you the tiger stalking its prey? Or is the tiger stalking you? If so, is there something in your life that you want to get rid of, perhaps an overinflated ego or a pattern of negativity?

turkey:

Whether it's alive or cooked, a turkey is a symbol of abundance. Relates to Thanksgiving, family gatherings, and overeating—as in "gobble, gobble." Alternately, a dim-witted person.

turtle:

Protection, security, long life, steady progress. Relates to a sense of being in a shell, withdrawn from life, blocking your emotions. However, some turtles can move from water to land, which symbolizes an ability to shift easily between the unconscious and conscious. Look at the other images in the dream for clarification.

whale:

A dream of this enormous mammal might indicate that you are dealing with a whale of a project or idea. On the other hand, a whale dream may suggest you are overwhelmed. A whale that dives deep suggests a deepening exploration of the unconscious or emotions.

wolf:

In Native American lore, the wolf is good medicine, a symbol of the pathfinder, a teacher with great wisdom and knowledge. Dreaming of a wolf can be a sign of good things to come. Alternately, the wolf can be a symbol of a lone male aggressively pursuing a young female, as in the fairy tale of Little Red Riding Hood.

apple:

A gift, as the one a student gives a teacher. Also a temptation or loss of innocence, as in the story of Adam and Eve and the Garden of Eden. In this sense, the apple can represent becoming aware of hidden impulses, developing worldly knowledge. In folklore, a symbol of fertility. A sign of great affection, as in "the apple of someone's eye." If apples are spilling and rolling away from you, you may have "upset the apple cart," in other words, disturbed the status quo.

B

baby:

Purity, innocence, a new beginning, a new project, a spiritual birthing. Also an idea that is just starting to form. As an archetype, the infant reminds us what we aimed to achieve in the beginning and how we have faired. For a teen, such a dream might reveal a fear of pregnancy at a young age. Alternately, it may relate to the needs of your inner child or a desire to hold onto childlike ways.

baseball:

Teamwork, camaraderie, power, organization. Hitting a home run, succeeding, a victory. Getting things started, as in "play ball." Also an escape into a pleasurable activity, as in "take me out to the ball game." Alternately, a failure or dismissal as in "Strike three, you're out!"

basement:

Making a connection with the unconscious. Possibly you are unearthing something hidden in your past that you need to examine. Is the basement dark or well lit? A dark basement suggests you need to look inward. What's in the basement? Is it covered with cobwebs or in good order? A flooded basement might indicate rising emotions that you've suppressed. Lost animals in the basement could relate to creative efforts that have been pushed aside. A cluttered basement suggests a need to establish order or clean up the past.

blood:

The life force, love, passion, fire. Also connections to mother, "the voice of the blood." Drinking blood suggests brotherhood.

The blood of Christ symbolizes communion, a universal healing power. Loss of blood relates to a loss of love. Losing a lot of blood suggests a loss of power or a change for the worse regarding your fortunes. A transfusion suggests an increase in vitality.

C

camera:

Stopping the action. A desire to slow your life down, preserve the moment. Alternately, an effort to analyze something. What are you photographing? For someone who recently spent hours taking photos, such a dream is most likely the mind's way of processing the day's events.

camping:

Getting back in touch with the earth, the outdoors, wilderness. Embarking on a quest, an initiation, undergoing a test. A dream of camping in the wilderness might symbolize the beginning of a spiritual quest. Alternatively, if the experience is unpleasant, you might fear losing your home. Maybe you feel like you're roughing it in some aspect of your life.

candles:

Usually suggest something of a spiritual nature, a spiritual light, illumination. Also a sense of mystery, romance, the spell of the supernatural. A candle provides light in the dark or guidance through dark matters or through the unknown. If a candle burns down to nothing, it might indicate a fear or concern about death. A candle being put out, or "burning a candle at both ends," could indicate a feeling of being overworked. A steadily burning candle may signify a steadfast character and constancy in friends and family.

car:

If you're behind the wheel, it suggests that you're in control of a matter. You're moving ahead in your journey or toward your goal. Where are you headed? Who's with you? Is there something special or unique about the car? Are you going particularly fast or slow? If you're old enough to drive, but someone else is driving, it might suggest that you're being controlled. An accident might be an expression of your fears and anxieties, of being vulnerable or out of control. Such a dream might be a premonition, especially if it's particularly vivid. If you're driving erratically, be aware of any careless habits or reckless behavior on your part or on the part of others that might lead to misfortune.

classroom:

The learning process, gaining knowledge, personal growth. Why are you there? Is there a positive feeling about the environment? What are you learning? Are you being tested? Are you prepared?

clouds:

Dark, stormy clouds rolling in at a low altitude with flashing lightning may represent your anger regarding a situation. A slate-gray sky might indicate that your views are clouded on a subject. What is it in your life that needs clarity? Dreaming of white billowing clouds against a blue sky suggests that matters are clearing up.

clown:

The appearance of a clown in a dream might indicate that you need to lighten up, act silly, and not take everything so seriously. Alternately, it could be a warning that you might be acting in a foolish manner in some part of your life.

D

dancing:

Movement, energy, release of emotions, expression of joy, sensuality. Also ritual dance, which is a symbol of praise, a sacred dance. Alternately, trying to keep up, as in "I'm dancing as fast as I can." Changing partners in a dance might symbolize the end of a relationship. Such dreams also can be a way of expressing joy or sorrow, possibly about your body. In traditional societies, major life events are depicted and celebrated in dances. If you're dancing with a partner, it suggests that you may be working in harmony or relating well to the person. If you're dancing and your partner isn't, the suggestion might be that you need to move with care, as in "dancing around" a certain person or matter.

darkness:

Symbol of your shadow side. Fear of the unknown, of people and things you don't understand. As a metaphor, what are you "in the dark" about? If you dream of working in a darkroom, you might be delving into a mystery, seeking answers, exploring the unknown. Something is developing, or you are in self-development, entering a spiritual quest.

devil:

Rigid aspects of your personality, guilt, temptation. Also avoidance, as in "the devil made me do it." A dream of the devil might reflect your fear of other beliefs that differ from your own. For some people who follow rigid religious systems, a fear might exist that the dreaming self is a demon rather than a source of inspiration and wisdom, and that the collective unconscious is the devil's realm.

door:

A common dream symbol, doors can indicate an opening or a new opportunity. Is the door open only a crack, or is it wide open waiting for you to enter? A closed door suggests that something is inaccessible or hidden. If a door is broken, there may be something hindering you from taking up a new opportunity. The condition of the door, including the material it's made of, and any markings that appear on it often provide clues about what lies behind a closed door. A doorman might be a pun for someone who can open doors for you.

E

earth:

Mother Earth, the Greek goddess Gaia, grounded, supportive, stable, our home. The earth is feminine and receptive. If you dream of looking down at the earth, you may be losing connection with something that is grounded and stable, possibly your roots, family, or culture. This symbol could also relate to something exotic or bizarre, like "nothing on earth" or "out of this world." Also a genuine, well-grounded person is "down to earth."

encyclopedia:

Inner knowledge, the collective unconscious, wisdom. An ability to remember, as in an "encyclopedic memory." If someone hands you a book in a dream, it's a gift of knowledge. If you're holding an encyclopedia, all the resources you need are at hand.

examination:

If you're taking an exam, it probably reflects some sort of test you're facing in your daily life. If in your dream you show up for class and realize that you haven't studied for an exam, it suggests a concern about not being prepared. In this common dream scenario, you might have forgotten to attend class until the day of the final exam. Sometimes called the student dream, you might still be having it many years after you're out of school. These dreams generally occur when we feel concerned about an upcoming event, such as a presentation, a speech, or a performance. See "Classroom."

f

feather:

Flight, connection with the heavens, the divine. In Native American cultures, feathers were sacred and related to healing and other rituals. In particular, an eagle feather represents strength, pride, protection, and transformation. A peacock feather represents beauty and insight. Alternately signifies escape, taking flight. Also achievement, as in "a feather in your cap."

feet:

Look what they do. They hold you up, like a foundation. Feet keep you grounded. Bare feet might suggest making contact. Footprints are about making an impression.

fire:

As one of the four elements, fire is masculine and aggressive. Highly emotional, psychic energy, also flaring anger. Being engulfed in flames, especially those that don't seem to frighten you, may be a symbol of spiritual growth, transformation, the divine fire burning within.

fish:

Going deep into the self, swimming in the spiritual depth. Large, colorful fish may suggest spiritual inspiration. The fish is a symbol of Christianity. In astrology, Pisces, a water sign, is linked to spring and birth as well as intuition, sensitivity, and gut instincts. According to Jung, fish are symbolic of wholeness and rebirth. A fish flopping on land could mean that you feel as if you're "a fish out of water" or "out of your depth."

fishing:

What did you catch? A stringer of fish could indicate luck. A large fish suggests a big catch of some sort. Catching fish can be a sign of fertility.

flag:

A signal alerting you to something significant or important. Flags can also be a symbol of pride or patriotism. Is someone trying to get your attention by flagging you down?

flashlight:

A light in the darkness, hope, a search for truth. (See "Lantern.") If someone is blinking a flashlight at you, it suggests that your unconscious is attempting to get your attention. It could also indicate a flash of inspiration, illumination.

flood:

Intense emotions, high anxiety. This symbol may relate to a feeling of anxiety about a situation that may be overwhelming you, as in trying to "keep your head above water." Could also signify the release of such feelings, as in "opening the floodgates."

food:

A table filled with food symbolizes abundance and fertility. Likewise, a table with hardly any food, accompanied by a sense of hunger, suggests concerns of poverty and lack. Fresh food, especially fruits and vegetables, may represent a sense of renewal. Food that is spoiled or rotting suggests waste and misuse of assets.

frog:

Fertility, creativity, and transformation. Dreaming of a frog might suggest that you are ready to move on to a new phase of your life. It also could indicate that you are about to take a big leap into something new. Tadpoles relate to children, childish ideas, growth, and potential. A dream of a frog also can relate to the idea of inner beauty as opposed to outer appearances, as in the fairy tale of the frog prince.

J

gambling:
It's about taking a risk. Look at the surrounding circumstances to decide if the risk is worthwhile. Keep in mind that those who don't take risks rarely achieve much of lasting value. On the other hand, if you see yourself losing at a gambling table, weigh the risk carefully before proceeding.

gold:
High value, success, "good as gold." Everything comes your way; you're the "golden boy" or "golden girl." Anything of great value, whether it's material, emotional, or spiritual worth.

green:
Growth, an increase in money. A prominent color in nature. Someone who is young or inexperienced. A green light also may signal a go-ahead, as with traffic lights.

grey:
Unformed or just taking shape, confusion, contradiction, a mixture of light and dark. The border between day and night, light and darkness.

H

hermit:
Personification of inner wisdom. An archetypal figure, he stands alone on his spiritual quest. If he's holding a lantern, he may be shedding light on a situation in your life that needs clarity. The light can also stand for inner light, enlightenment.

The hermit might represent a need to retreat to a private space or a withdrawal from mainstream society to make contact with nature and beauty. Alternately, the hermit can stand for a feeling of being isolated, lacking intimate relationships.

hiding place:

An escape from problems, a symbol of the unconscious. Alternately, a wish to be discovered.

home:

A feeling of security, comfort, a place of fond memories, as in "Home is where the heart is." A dream of your home may represent the self or anything of great value to you, such as your values, your family, or your wishes and desires. What does it look like? Is it dark or well-lit? Dreams of former homes might represent the person you were or the relationships you maintained when you lived there. What was it about yourself from that time that you wish to regain? Are you doing something now the way you did it in the past without realizing it?

house:

It might symbolize some part of you. Examine the house closely. Notice the number of rooms and the furnishings. Is it new or old, elegant or shabby? A new house might symbolize new beginnings, while an old house may signify that you're sticking to old ways. An attic may be a place where you are hiding part of yourself. A basement might symbolize a connection to the unconscious. Upper rooms might give you perspective on your life, while bedrooms relate to intimacy or personal matters.

I

ice:

Ice may symbolize the emotional state of the dreamer or a person in the dream. Are you receiving an "icy reception"? If the ice is melting, maybe a cold relationship is getting warmer. If you're in a shaky situation, you could be "skating on thin ice." In a romantic context, ice means lack of desire. To dream of ice floating in a clear stream signifies an interruption of happiness, while dreaming of eating ice portends illness. A dream of an iceberg indicates that you're being blocked everywhere you turn.

ice cream:

Obstacles are being removed, and there is reason to celebrate. If ice cream is your favorite dessert, the dream indicates that you're being rewarded or there's reason to treat yourself.

insects:

If it's a "creepy, crawly" insect, it might relate to fears and annoyances, particularly with difficult people. What's annoying or "bugging" you? Feelings of insignificance, getting stepped on. Stinging insects suggest "stinging remarks."

ants:

Feeling restless, antsy. Small annoyances, irritations, stinging results, anxiety. Alternately, a dream of ants may represent feelings of smallness or insignificance. Also, industrious, hardworking, or working together.

bees:

Well organized, working together, buzzing about. A need to be part of a community or to get your life organized. Overworked, "busy as a bee." A single buzzing bee might relate to gossip. In mythology, bees are messengers of the gods, a connection with the divine. Also status or rank, as in the need to be the "queen bee." Honey in legend is the elixir of the gods. If you are seeking honey, it suggests you need to add more sweetness to your life. Or maybe you are seeking a "honey."

bug:

Annoyances, petty disturbances. Getting "bugged." Also, bothersome information, as in a "bug in your ear." A need for change, as in "going buggy." Also, since bugs are a term for small devices used in spying, a bug could relate to a concern about being watched or spied upon.

butterfly:

Lightness, beauty, transformation, rebirth. Alternately, are you flitting about like a butterfly, moving from group to group, lacking commitment, stability, or failing to get your work done?

spider:

Taking a careful and energetic approach to your work. A symbol that you will be pleasantly rewarded for your labors. To dream of a spider spinning its web signifies that your home life will be happy and secure. Many spiders represent good health and friends. In folklore, a confrontation with a large spider may signify a quick climb to fame and fortune, unless the large spider bites you, in which case it may represent the loss of money or reputation. Alternately, especially in a man's dream, a female spider can represent a devouring mother, the feminine power to possess or ensnare.

island:

An exotic place, an isolated getaway. Being cut off from the rest of the world. Possibly a vacation is due. Finding yourself on a deserted island suggests you are isolating yourself from others or from your inner self.

J

jaws:

Do you feel like you're under attack? Such a dream might also relate to a disagreement, as in someone giving you a "lot of jaw." Or, if it's your jaws, you may be the aggressor. Jaws also can represent the entry point to a journey into the underworld.

juggling:

Keeping your options open, balancing the many facets of your life. Do you have an audience? Are you being judged? How well are you doing with your juggling act, and how is the audience reacting?

jumping:

Taking a chance, leaping into the void, a need for more excitement. A new start, as in the "jumping-off point." You might be concerned about getting or staying "one jump ahead."

jungle:

The hidden, dark part of the self that you've been avoiding. Your unconscious may be telling you of a need to explore this part of yourself. If you're on a quest in search of treasure, the jungle may symbolize a great, uncharted part of you that is ripe for spiritual growth. Also confusion and a potential threat, as in "It's a jungle out there."

jury:

If you're on a jury, it may be time to make an important decision in your life. If you find yourself on trial before a jury, it indicates a concern or anxiety about the reaction of family or friends about a decision you've made. Also feelings of guilt or feeling that you are on trial. Are people judging you?

key:

It opens a door and allows you to enter your home. Finding a key relates to gaining access, new knowledge. If you lose a key, it relates to a change in living circumstances that causes a feeling of loss.

killing:

If you kill someone, it's probably not a warning that you might turn into a killer. Instead, the meaning is more likely a symbolic act of aggression. Whom did you kill, and how is that person involved in your life? If you don't recognize the person, the dream may symbolize killing off an unwanted part of yourself, possibly your shadow side. If you are on a spiritual path, the dream could represent a desire to kill your ego.

kidnapping:

Victimized, a loss of power, losing control, feeling trapped. Is someone restricting your freedom or growth? If you cooperate with your captors, you may be feeling that someone should take control of a part of your life.

king:

Seeking status, authority, or support, a need to control. The height of male power and authority. He can be benevolent or cruel. The king may represent your father or some other powerful figure in your life, someone you look up to or admire, or someone you fear. If you're the king, it might indicate that you have achieved a high level of authority or are a highly capable individual.

kiss:

A variety of meanings, depending on the circumstances, ranging from devotion and romance to betrayal. Metaphors range in variation from "kiss and make up" to "kiss of death." A "kiss off" spells the end of something. Is it dark or light out during the kiss? The former suggests danger or an illicit situation, while the latter represents honorable intentions. To dream of kissing someone on the neck suggests passionate feelings regarding a matter at hand or a wish to suck energy from the person.

kitchen:

What's cooking? Is the kitchen cluttered and disorganized? Are you cooking several things simultaneously, or are you out of food? You might think of the kitchen as a place of creativity and nurturing. But if you consider the kitchen as a place of drudgery, the dream might take on a negative meaning.

L

laboratory:

Experimenting with life, dealing with our emotions. The implication is that the dreamer is unsatisfied with a present situation and is experimenting with something new. The dreamer might also be weighing a relationship, as in "testing the waters."

labyrinth:

Feeling trapped in a situation or relationship and looking for a way out. Labyrinths are also symbolic of a spiritual journey, winding inward toward your inner self. How you feel inside the labyrinth determines the nature of the dream. Encountering beasts in the labyrinth suggests that enemies or competitors are blocking your path. Looking down upon a labyrinth from above suggests that you are preparing to embark on a spiritual quest.

lagoon:

The still waters are a powerful symbol of female energy, especially when the dreamer is male. Alternately, doubts and confusion over an emotional matter or a stagnant situation.

lamb:

Innocence and vulnerability, as in "a lamb to the slaughter." Are you acting "meek as a lamb"? Is someone trying to "pull the wool over your eyes"? It may also be a spiritual symbol as a "sacrificial lamb" or "lamb of God." Alternately, a dream of a lamb might just suggest a love of animals.

ladder:

Achievement, as in climbing the ladder to success. Each rung might suggest a level of achievement or your place within an organization. Alternately, a ladder might relate to a union with the divine—as with Jacob's Ladder, leading into heaven—a connection with the unconscious below and the conscious above. Are you climbing up or down the ladder?

lantern:

A light shining in the darkness, illumination, a search for truth or honesty, like the legendary Greek figure, Diogenes, who carried a lantern in daylight searching for an honest man.

lap:

A symbol of security, as in the "lap of luxury." Sitting on someone's lap signifies safety from some troubling matter. A cat curled in a lap represents danger from a seductive enemy.

late:

To dream of arriving late could relate to anxieties about deadlines, missed opportunities. If you're worried in your dream about catching a plane or train, it suggests a concern about reaching a goal.

laughing:

A message from the unconscious that you need to stop brooding. Such dreams often result in a shift of moods from sadness and tension to lightheartedness. Did others laugh with you? Did you feel a sense of relief? If someone was laughing *at* you, it might reflect feelings of inadequacy, fear, or guilt.

Alternately, you may be laughing at yourself. Are you taking yourself too seriously?

lawyer:
Related to justice, legal matters, possibly a divorce. If you've been involved in such a situation, the dream might be reflecting your anxieties. Lawyers can also mean that you need to make a decision on some matter. Also consider your feelings about lawyers. The image could be either a positive or negative one, depending on your perspective.

lightning:
A flash of inspiration, an indication that the truth about a troubling matter will soon be revealed. Getting hit by lightning symbolizes sudden change inspired by new knowledge that struck you "like a bolt of lightning." Lightning can also mean a purge or purification, or fear of authority or death. Alternately, lightning can symbolize a warning of danger.

m

magic:
In the dream world, you exist outside of space and time, and you acquire supernatural abilities. You can walk through walls, instantly move from one place to another, change your appearance, or even become another person. In a lucid dream state, the ability becomes exhilarating because you are directing the action. These abilities may be an inherent part of your dream state, or you may gain them by picking up an object of power. Possessing such talents in your dreams is your unconscious

mind's way of telling you that you have the innate abilities to solve your problems, to make your dreams come true. Such a dream might also be a reaction to feeling powerless in your daily life.

mail:

A message is on the way. Someone might be trying to contact you. Alternately, your unconscious might be sending you a message. It may relate to your need to communicate with others and make sure they get your message. Is there an unresolved matter in your life that requires you to contact others? Mail could be a pun on "male," as in a new male figure is entering your life.

magnet:

If it looks like a horseshoe, it might mean good luck. It can also symbolize something or someone that attracts your attention, draws you near, or influences you. On the other hand, it might relate to envy of someone who is charismatic and who attracts attention away from you.

map:

A search for a new path. Seeking a new direction or new goals. Your unconscious might be alerting you to changes in the air, or you might soon be looking for a change of direction. If you're guiding someone else with the map, it may reflect a desire for more influence. If someone else has the map, it may suggest that you need more direction.

marathon:

A long way to go, running the distance, an ability to succeed at difficult tasks. If you're not a marathon runner in your waking life, a dream of running in one symbolizes a daunting goal. How are you doing in the dream? Are you falling behind, or are you passing the competition? Do you feel strong, or is your energy flagging?

merry-go-round:

Going round and round about something. Repetitious behavior, making no progress. Going in circles, getting nowhere fast. If you enjoy the experience, you need to consider why you like going around in circles. Also relates to cyclical matter, such as the seasons, and feminine energy.

meteor:

A wish upon a star, wishful thinking. Also a message from heaven, inspiration, or a gift from the gods.

monster:

Often associated with nightmares, a frightening being or beast often indicates that you are afraid of facing something within you that needs to change. Also an internal conflict or, especially for a child, fear of changes or new elements in one's environment, the need to grow and change. If you have recurring dreams about monsters, it's best to confront the creature rather than run away in fear. Facing the monster usually diminishes its threatening nature, and it even may run from you.

moon:

Related to feminine energy or mystique and creativity. Also emotions, intuition, psychic realms, the imagination, and the yin principal (as in yin and yang). The moon can also relate matters of cyclical nature, a rising tide or force, the pull of dark, mysterious desires, a sensual and overpowering attraction. The moon can symbolize your mother and the relationship between mother and child.

N

nail:

Putting something together, "nailing it down." If you "hit the nail on the head," you're on target. If you've broken a fingernail, the dream might relate to a concern about handling details in your life.

needle:

Sewing things together, especially if there is thread along with the needle. Finishing a matter, completing a project. Threading a needle relates to dealing with details. If needles are sticking in your skin, it might relate to acupuncture. Are you undergoing a healing process, or are you sick and in need of healing? Needles sticking in a doll, like a voodoo doll, might symbolize someone taking some action against you. Metaphors include an impossible situation, as in "looking for a needle in a haystack." Also feeling under attack, as in the case of someone "needling you."

nest:

Home, or a desire to return there, possibly to the place where you grew up. If you are moving, it might relate to your concern about your new home. If there is an egg in the nest, the dream might relate to a concern about your savings or "nest egg."

nose:

A symbol of intrusive behavior, as in "sticking one's nose into someone else's business." Dreaming of a nose suggests that someone is interfering in your life, but it could also mean that *you* are being nosy.

numbers:

Often symbolic in dreams, relating to universal meanings of the numbers, especially zero through ten. They also can hold personal meaning, such as the date and year of your birth or the birth date of someone important in your life. Also other significant dates: anniversaries, holiday, number of children, or siblings. Here are meanings of individual numbers.

0:

The most mysterious of numbers, it is nothing and something at the same time. It has many possible interpretations. Zero can mean emptiness, a lack of something in your life. It also forms a circle and can stand for wholeness and completion, or even the mysteries of the unknown.

1:

The starting point, pioneering, initiating. Unity. Making a decision, selecting the one. Uniqueness, as in "I'm Number One." Wholeness, the cosmic divinity, the One. The ultimate spiritual level.

2:

Cooperation, adaptability, partnership. Alternately, the number relates to opposite poles, including male/female, conscious/unconscious, dark/light, intellect/emotions. A dream featuring the number two suggests a need for balance. Two can represent either a marriage or pairing of opposites.

3:

Expression, verbalization, socialization, the arts. Also tension, as in "Three's a crowd." Three correlates with a triangle and trinity, a sacred religious symbol, and is also linked to mind, body, and soul.

4:

Foundation, order, service, struggling against limits, steady growth. Also, the earth, stability, strength. The four elements—earth, air, water, and fire.

5:

In numerology, the number usually relates to expansiveness, visionary, the constructive use of freedom, searching, an adventure. Human consciousness, the five senses.

6:

In numerology, the number represents responsibility, protection, nurturing, community, balance. Symmetry, unity of spirit and body, a harmonious relationship.

7:

A spiritual number, the seven colors of the rainbow, the seven vices, the seven days of the week, the seven virtues, the seven planets of early astrology, the seven chakras, the seven veils. A sense of wholeness, becoming your true self.

8:

Dreaming of the number might relate to possession, status, or money. Also practical endeavors and power-seeking, and a symbol of wholeness, completion. An eight tipped over on its side is the mathematical symbol for infinity.

9:

In numerology, the number relates to humanitarian deeds, selflessness, creative endeavors, obligations. Also pregnancy, childbirth. The end of a cycle and the start of something new.

O

oak:

An oak tree, a sacred symbol in Celtic lore, represents strength, stability, endurance, truth, and wisdom. A dream with an oak may suggest that a strong, proper foundation has been established in a matter.

oar:

Masculinity and strength. If it dips into water, it suggests that emotional matters involving a male figure are coming to a head. To row vigorously suggests a need for aggressiveness or that you are moving through an issue. If you've lost an oar and are rowing in circles, it might suggest frustration at the lack of forward movement.

ocean:

Emotional depth, infinity, the collective unconscious. The ocean is also associated with the womb and the mother. Carl Jung saw the ocean as the realm of emotional life.

p

park:

A wish to relax and enjoy life. Walking in an unlit park at night may mean that you are delving into areas of darkness and danger or that you are dealing with hidden or mysterious matters. As a metaphor, a park may suggest that you are not moving ahead, as being "in park" or parked.

photograph:

A memory, a captured moment, a symbol of being caught up or mentally trapped in the past. Looking back. Also a desire to be remembered. A dream of a photo of yourself indicates introspection, a desire to look inward. A developing picture indicates something is coming into focus or coming into being.

piano:

Coming into harmony with various facets of your life. Getting yourself in tune with those around you, especially if the piano is out of tune.

pilot:

Someone who soars high and remains in control. Are you in the pilot's seat concerning some issue in your life? This symbol differs from a flying dream in that you are responsible and controlling the craft, which is a metaphor for rising above your problems but not ignoring them. If you're holding a handheld computer (a "Palm Pilot"), it indicates a wish to control or "pilot" something. If another person is holding the Palm Pilot, it may reflect a concern that someone is controlling you.

planets:

If you're traveling to another planet, it suggests a need to escape. Seeing planets in alignment in the sky suggests a cosmic, spiritual, or universal theme, an exploration of the vast beyond. Dreams of seeing a specific planet in our solar system may relate to the astrological energy attributed to that heavenly body.

Mercury:

Rapid communication, messages, quick thinking. In Greek mythology, Hermes.

Venus:

Love and affection, the goddess of love, deep emotions. It's also about what you value.

Mars:

Aggression, warlike mentality, initiative, courage, male energy. In Greek mythology, Ares.

Jupiter:

Philosophy, higher education, expansion, and integration. Growth and prosperity. Opportunity, luck, and higher mind. Related to Zeus in Greek mythology.

Saturn:

Responsibilities, karma, discipline, limitations and restrictions. Related to Chronos in Greek mythology.

Uranus:

Sudden unexpected disruptions. Breaks with tradition. Related to the Greek god Ouranos.

Neptune:

Spiritual insight, illusion. Imagination, dreams, psychic experience, unconscious influences. God of the sea. Associated with Poseidon, the earth shaker, in Roman mythology.

Pluto:

Relates to extremes. Also death and rebirth. Getting to the core of something. Transformation. Associated with Hades in Roman mythology.

pyramid:

Something ancient and mysterious. A source of power and wonder. An enigma. Also a source of virility and creativity, or a symbol of resurrection, a place between Earth and Heaven. On a more mundane level, a pyramid might be symbolic of an urge for adventure travel.

Q

quarantine:

Seeing yourself quarantined might relate to a need for a spiritual cleansing or renewal. You are isolated for your own good. Alternately, the dream might be a warning that you need to take care of yourself to avoid illness.

quarrel:

Repressed anger or inner turmoil coming to the surface. If the person you're arguing with is identifiable, see if you can pinpoint the area of disagreement. There could be clues in the dream that indicate a way of resolving the differences.

queen:

Power and authority. Her court is composed of the people around her, whether it's her family or her coworkers. The queen archetype also is linked to arrogance, aggression, and emotional behavior. As such, the dark queen is seen as a wicked force, especially in fairy tales. Dreaming that you are a queen might relate to issues of control and authority that can be used in either a benevolent or destructive manner. The Ice Queen rules with cold indifference. The Queen Bee empowers the hive, but everyone must serve her.

rabbit:

A symbol of fertility and magic, as in pulling a rabbit from a hat. It might also concern financial abundance, the success of a particular project. A white rabbit may signify purity or faithfulness in love.

radio:

Something in the air, something new, messages, new ideas, communicating. If you see or hear yourself on the radio in a dream, it may indicate that you have something to say that's important and worthwhile.

rain:

A fresh downpour symbolizes a washing or cleansing away of the old. A fresh start, something sparkling, new growth. Alternately, dark skies and a gloomy situation. Is someone "raining on your parade"? To hear the patter of rain on the roof suggests domestic bliss, while watching a downpour from inside a house may represent security and fortune. Also abundance and anything on a grand scale: "When it rains, it pours."

rainbow:

Favorable conditions, a resolution after a time of unpleasant-ness. Finding the pot of gold at the end of the rainbow. Wishing for a pot of gold or the equivalent. A symbol of success in your endeavors, luck.

raincoat:

Protection against rampant emotions, a downpour of anger or discontent.

road:

A connection between one point and another. What is the condition of the road in your dream? Is it smooth and fast or bumpy and slow? The former suggests easy going ahead. The latter warns that you can expect delays and minor annoyances. If the road dips and curves, it may indicate that you need to be aware, flexible, and ready for change. A roadblock or detour suggests that you may encounter unexpected changes in your plans.

robe:

Changing your ways, in transition, cleansing, as in wearing a robe after a bath or while getting ready to put on new or different clothes. Also a religious symbol, something sacred, or something from the past. A matter that is covered, hidden in the unconscious, that might be exposed at any time.

roller coaster:

Emotional ups and downs, especially if there is also water in the dream. Also rapid movement or communication, but with some scary moments in the process. "It's like a roller coaster ride!"

rope:

Restrictions, a knotty situation. Something holding you back. Are you feeling all tied up or tied down? Did you get "roped into" doing something you didn't want to do? Look at some of the other metaphors that might fit your situation. Is someone giving you "enough rope to hang yourself"? If that fits, the message is caution. Or maybe you "know the ropes." You realize that you are an authority on a matter. If your "hands are tied," the dream suggests that you're limited in how you can respond to a situation. If frustration is the issue, you may be "at the end of your rope."

rose:

A symbol of the feminine, associated with romance. A dream of someone handing you a rose may indicate an offering of love. A rose can also relate to good and evil. A crushed rose suggests someone's ill intentions.

shoes:

Grounded, protection. Shoes also represent one's personal characteristics. To dream of taking off your shoes suggests leaving behind the past, dropping a way of acting or a role, being open to change. Your dreaming self might also be letting you know that you need to be more empathetic toward others, as in "walking in someone else's shoes for a day." Also accepting a role or way of life, as in "If the shoe fits, wear it."

snake:

An archetypal image that can have numerous interpretations, both positive and negative, from healing powers and wisdom to devious behavior and demons. In mythology, snakes are symbols of wisdom, of healing and fertility, and of renewal, as seen in the shedding of their skin. Snakes can also symbolize the dangers of the underworld. In Christianity, the snake stands for temptation and the source of evil. In some Eastern traditions, the snake is related to a power that rises from the base of the spine and can be a sign of transformation. Snakes can suggest feelings of deviousness, as in "a snake in the grass." A winding, twisting snake, as in the caduceus—the emblem that signifies a doctor's or medical office—represents healing. The way you view snakes symbolically, along with other aspects of the dream, should guide you in your interpretation. In mythology, the snake climbing a tree symbolizes the process of becoming conscious, a variation on the Adam and Eve story.

secret:

If you're keeping a secret in a dream, it might relate to body changes taking place at puberty or anything that you're not ready to reveal about yourself.

star:

A symbol of higher awareness, a feeling about your destiny, as in "It's in the stars." A metaphor for a celebrity, a brightly shining star in your dream could point to a desire to be noticed.

storm:

Emotional turmoil. An approaching storm indicates building tension. Dark skies and thunder may also be a forewarning that danger is approaching. Alternately, a storm could signal that rapid and dramatic changes are occurring in your life.

strangers:

An element in your personality that you don't know very well on the conscious level. A stranger, especially one who threatens or upsets you, may represent your fears or an attitude or behavior that you should keep out of your life. Depending on the actions of the stranger, he or she might represent an institution you fear, such as a prison or a hospital.

T

table:

The search for a firm foundation. A symbol of social gatherings, family matters. A meeting of minds. The condition and quality of the table represent the quality of your relationships with family members. Note if there is anything on top of the table. To dream of an empty table suggests a concern about the lack or shortage of possessions. A table covered with food represents a wish for abundance or that abundance has arrived.

tattoo:

A symbol of protection, identification, allegiance, a need for attention. Making a strong impression. For more clues, look at the shape of the tattoo, the color, and its location on the body.

telephone:

Making contact, connections or misconnections, miscommunication. Contact with the unconscious. If the phone is ringing and no one is answering, the dream might suggest that you are ignoring the call of your unconscious. But the meaning of the dream depends on what happens with the telephone. If you make contact with an old friend or a deceased loved one, the dream could be about your desire for a reunion or a return to conditions of the past. On the other hand, if the telephone doesn't work, it suggests a failure of communication in your life. If the phone works, but the person you reach is uncooperative, the dream indicates that you might be dealing with the wrong people regarding a situation in your life. It could also mean that you're frustrated about a lack of enthusiasm or cooperation on the part of someone about something that's important to you.

television:

Viewing your life or some aspect of it from a distance. Remaining detached but in control. Do you hold the remote control? Alternately, seeing yourself on television might signal acclaim, recognition, accomplishments.

test:

You find yourself in class and realize that you haven't studied for the test. You may have forgotten to attend classes for the entire semester. If you've had this dream, you're not alone. It's one of the common dream themes and usually relates to concerns about being unprepared for something that's coming up in your daily life. See "Examination."

thief:

Something is being taken from you, or you feel that's the case. Is someone stealing your energy? If you're the thief, the message is that you're being warned that you're taking what you don't deserve and that you should change your ways. Also a fear of loss in a personal relationship that is souring.

toes:

Attending to details, paying close attention to minor points. Where in your daily life do you deal with details? Whether the dream is negative or positive will be determined by the other elements in the dream.

trees:

Abundance, fertility, happiness, growth. Also protection, a symbol of life. The health of the tree mirrors the mental or psychological health of the dreamer or the people in the dream.

Trees can also serve as an intermediary between heaven and earth. Is the tree healthy and vibrant or wilted and sick? Is someone going to cut it down? Can you identify the tree and attach a sense of personality to it? Is it strong like an oak, flexible like a willow, or prickly like a pine? Are you taking a chance, as in "out on a limb"?

U

UFO:

Something hidden within the self or something transforming within you. A UFO reveals that you are more than what is evident. An enormous UFO filling the sky reveals the wondrous nature of the self and your role in creation. See "Alien."

umbrella:

Protection against adverse conditions or an emotional flood from the unconscious. If the umbrella is closed and you're getting soaked by a downpour, the indication is that you are exposed to your emotional needs.

unicycle:

Keeping everything in balance. Alternately, you're the big wheel and you're on your own.

V

vampire:

A mythic creature associated with bloodsucking and erotic behavior. To see yourself as a vampire suggests that you lust for their power or position or for their physical strength and shape-shifting abilities. It might also be a symbolic image related to the male-female relationship in which one partner drains the power of the other for his or her own psychic survival. Once bitten, the victim submits, even though being bitten means eventually losing all power. Is something or someone draining you of energy? Is someone taking advantage of you? The message is to guard against people who take too much of your time and energy. To dream of battling a vampire or driving a stake through its heart suggests a positive outcome against someone with harmful intentions.

vegetables:

A symbol of nourishment, harvest, abundance. An onion can represent a complicated matter that's gradually being exposed. A tuber, such as a potato, can symbolize deep roots, connections with the unconscious. As a metaphor, vegetables suggest that you are vegetating, relaxing, or growing stagnant.

victim:

Feeling victimized. Your dreaming self might be telling you that some behavior on your part must be altered or released. If you are the victim, pay attention to the perpetrators. Find out what decision you made or actions you took that led to the situation. How do you feel about the role? Are you upset, or do you enjoy it? How does it relate to events in your waking life? Are you rewarded with sympathy when you are a victim? Alternately, the dream might relate to your tendency to victimize others for personal gain. To make good use of the dream, you must recognize your role in the scenario, as either victim or perpetrator, and decide how you can remedy the situation.

volcano:

Emotional release, letting go, or healing old wounds. The eruption of a volcano may represent suppressed urges, fears, and anger or personal revelations breaking into your conscious mind. A healing process that can be disturbing. A smoldering volcano suggests things are about to erupt in your life. Possibly a big break of some kind or other life-changing events are about to explode.

W

water:

Relates to the unconscious, emotions, and the depth of your being. A stormy sea relates to turbulent emotions, illusion, and chaos. A tranquil sea, on the other hand, suggests placid feelings. A flood or high water can represent a rise in unconscious energy. Finding yourself beneath the waves indicates that you're immersed in your emotions. Water also can represent a living essence of the life energy, refreshment.

waterfalls:

A sudden change in the dreamer's emotions, a fear of being overwhelmed by activity in the unconscious, a sense of danger. A plunge into the unknown, into turbulence.

weeds:

Something unwanted, an annoyance. Weeds might represent a part of your life that you've been overlooking that needs attention. Are the weeds growing high? Dying weeds might reveal that you are confronting a weakness and overcoming it.

wheel:

Symbolic of cycles, rotations. As a circular image with spokes radiating from the center, it represents a mandala, a sacred image of the self. Also a means of moving ahead, as in "wheeling and dealing." Someone who's in charge, a "big wheel."

wings:

A means of transport representing air travel. If the wings are attached to you, it could indicate that you'll be soaring high or that you're someone's angel. Wings also symbolize intuition, something sacred. Also escape, as in "taking wing." Are you attempting to rise above your problems? Or are you going to act without much preparation, as in "winging it"?

witch:

The way you see a witch affects the meaning of a dream in which one appears. The Halloween image of a witch might be symbolic of a scary or evil scenario. A witch might also relate to the worship and respect of nature and the earth. If you are casting a spell in the dream, you may be seeking power over someone or just attempting to attract his or her attention. Alternately, a dream that someone is casting a spell on you suggests that you're spellbound by someone in your life.

X

x rays:

A desire for inner knowledge, a yearning to explore the inner self. On the other hand, if you haven't been feeling well lately, the dream might be a warning that you need to get a checkup.

If someone else you know is getting x-rayed, the dream may suggest that you are "seeing through" this person, in other words, understanding what the person is about.

yellow:

Light, the sun, consciousness, higher awareness. Also legal matters, contracts. But a dream in which the color is dominant also might relate to a concern about cowardice, as in "a yellow streak," or worry about illness, as in "yellow fever."

Z

zipper:

Keeping everything together. Keeping quiet, as in "zip it up." If a zipper is stuck, it suggests feelings of frustration and incompetence.

zodiac:

If you are interested in astrology, a zodiac wheel might indicate a search for understanding, the deeper meaning of life. Seeing one particular sign, such as the Gemini twins or Taurus the bull, relates to the particular meaning of the sign. Does the sign represent anyone in your life? Who is showing you the sign?

zoo:

A dream of a zoo might relate to a feeling of being in a cage. It could also symbolize chaos, as in "This place is such a zoo." Alternately, it could recall a time of recreation and pleasure.

Appendix

Resources

ere is a list of books for those who are interested in continuing their research of dreams. Used copies of some of the older books might be found in Internet bookstores, such as Amazon.com or Barnes & Noble. You can also find a variety of Web sites on the Internet by searching with the key words "dreams," "dream interpretation," "dream research," "lucid dreaming," or "out-of-body experiences." To learn more about Edgar Cayce, go to *www.arecayce. com*, the site for the Association for Research and Enlightenment.

The Bedside Guide to Dreams, by Stase Michaels (Fawcett, 1995).

Cloud Nine: A Dreamer's Dictionary, by Sandra A. Thomson (Avon, 1994).

Conscious Dreaming: A Spiritual Path for Everyday Life, by Robert Moss (Crown, 1996).

Creative Dreaming, by Patricia Garfield (Ballantine, 1974).

The Dream Encyclopedia, by James R. Lewis (Visible Ink, 1995).

The Dream Game, by Ann Faraday (Harper and Row, 1976).

Dream Power, by Ann Faraday (Berkeley, 1981).

Dream Power: How to Use Your Night Dreams to Change Your Life, by Cynthia Richmond (Fireside, 2001).

Dreamwork for the Soul: A Spiritual Guide to Dream Interpretation, by Rosemary Ellen Guiley (Berkeley, 1998).

The Dream Workbook: Discover the Knowledge and Power Hidden in Your Dreams, by Jill Morris (Fawcett Crest, 1985).

Exploring the World of Lucid Dreaming, by Stephen LaBerge (Ballantine, 1990).

In Your Dreams, by Gayle Delaney (Harper Collins, 1997).

The Lucid Dream: A Waking Guide for the Travelers Between Worlds, by Malcolm Godwin (Simon & Schuster, 1994).

Lucid Dreaming: The Power of Being Awake & Aware in Your Dreams, by Stephen LaBerge (Ballantine, 1985).

Working with Dreams, by Montague Ullman and Nan Zimmerman (Dell, 1979).

Index